Free Video  Free Video

Essential Test Tips Video from Trivium Test Prep

Dear Customer,

Thank you for purchasing from Trivium Test Prep! We're honored to help you prepare for your APUSH exam.

To show our appreciation, we're offering a **FREE** *APUSH Essential Test Tips* **Video by Trivium Test Prep.*** Our video includes 35 test preparation strategies that will make you successful on the APUSH. All we ask is that you email us your feedback and describe your experience with our product. Amazing, awful, or just so-so: we want to hear what you have to say!

To receive your **FREE** *APUSH Essential Test Tips* **Video**, please email us at 5star@ triviumtestprep.com. Include "Free 5 Star" in the subject line and the following information in your email:

1. The title of the product you purchased.
2. Your rating from 1 – 5 (with 5 being the best).
3. Your feedback about the product, including how our materials helped you meet your goals and ways in which we can improve our products.
4. Your full name and shipping address so we can send your **FREE** *APUSH Essential Test Tips* **Video**.

If you have any questions or concerns please feel free to contact us directly at 5star@ triviumtestprep.com.

Thank you!

– Trivium Test Prep Team

*To get access to the free video please email us at 5star@triviumtestprep.com, and please follow the instructions above.

AP US History
Study Guide 2021-2022
Review Book with Practice Test Questions
for the Advanced Placement Exam

Table of Contents

Introduction

The Advanced Placement United States History (APUSH) examination covers the period from 1491 through the present era. This year, the College Board—the organization that administers all AP tests—has significantly increased the APUSH examination's focus on the time period between 1491 and 1607, as well as on the years after 1980. College Board changes to the curriculum and areas of focus are reflected in this guide.

Like other AP courses, individual teachers have a wide degree of freedom to cover topics and subjects of particular interest during the year-long course. The textbook assigned for your class may vary. Typically, any college-level American history textbook is acceptable for the APUSH course. The text should be supplemented with various materials, including primary sources, maps, scholarly works on U.S. history and artwork.

What does this mean for you? It means that your teacher may spend more or less time and attention on certain topics, which necessitates that you put in extra study time in order to gain a thorough understanding of the chronology and key topics you will encounter on the APUSH exam.

This study guide is not intended to take the place of a college-level textbook, and is not designed for students who are testing against the APUSH exam without first enrolling and completing the course. Rather, this guide serves as a broad, high-level overview of the material you will most likely encounter on the exam. As such, you would be wise to augment your preparation by studying your assigned textbook and reviewing any notes you took during class.

From time to time, you will see an icon like the one. That indicates that the information in this paragraph is critical to your success on the practice examinations. It's important to read everything to learn critical context, but when you come back to study, look for these paragraphs.

APUSH Skills and Thematic Objectives

The APUSH will test your mastery of the following skills:

1. Historical argumentation
2. Interpretation
3. Appropriate use of historical evidence
4. Historical causation
5. Patterns of change and continuity
6. Periodization
7. Comparison
8. Contextualization
9. Synthesis

The APUSH exam will also test your knowledge of the "thematic objectives" associated with this course. The purpose here is not to teach you to be able to recite historical facts, but to be able to use and apply historical knowledge in a variety of different ways. This study guide is organized chronologically and thematically – each period will cover several of the APUSH exam's thematic objectives. In the practice examinations at the back of the book, you will find specific questions that cover these objectives.

1. Identity
   a. Why and how have debates over the idea of an American identity shifted and changed over time?
   b. How have personal identities functioned in different eras?
2. Work, Exchange and Technology
   a. In what ways have technology, the marketplace, and transportation impacted or changed American society?
   b. How have labor systems impacted the development of American society, with a particular focus on the differences between British and North American labor systems?
   c. How have differences in economic ideologies and debates over economics impacted the environment, society, politics and the economy?
3. Peopling
   a. What reasons have led to migrations to North America, as well as from and within North America?
   b. In what ways have changing migration patterns and population affected life in America?
4. Politics and Power

a. Why and how have different groups fought for political, economic and social influence in the land that would become the United States and, later, the United States?

b. What values have guided American politics through time and how have Americans disagreed or argued about these values over time?

5. America in the World

a. In what ways have events in North America and/or the United States impacted global events and affairs?

b. What factors have impacted U.S. involvement in international affairs of various sorts, including diplomatic, military and political?

6. Environment and Geography: Physical and Human

a. How did the natural environment impact the behavior, beliefs and actions of the people living in the United States?

b. In what ways did the economic and demographic changes over time in the United States impact the surrounding environment, as well as discussions about use of the environment and resources?

7. Ideas, Beliefs and Culture

a. Why and how have cultural and moral beliefs and values in the United States changed over time?

b. How have these changes impacted American history over time?

The Course Breakdown

The APUSH course is broken down into nine distinct chronological periods. Below, you'll find information identifying each of these periods, as well as the percentage of class time in the course relating to this period. You should note, that in terms of the examination, periods 2 through 5 total 45 percent of the questions on the examination, and periods 6 through 8 total another 45 percent, with period 1 and period 9 each totaling 5 percent of the questions on the test. You will see that several periods overlap.

As you work through this book, you'll notice more information and more detail for periods that are heavily weighted on the examination, and less on those that are not as significant.

Period	Percentage of Test
Period 1: 1491-1607	5 percent
Period 2: 1607-1754	10 percent
Period 3: 1754-1800	12 percent
Period 4: 1800-1848	10 percent

Period	Percentage of Test
Period 5: 1844-1877	13 percent
Period 6: 1865-1898	13 percent
Period 7: 1890-1945	17 percent
Period 8: 1945-1980	15 percent
Period 9: 1980-present	5 percent

Later in this guide, you'll find explanations of the chronology of each period, as well as the key focuses of study for each.

Scoring

The test is scored on a scale of 1 to 5. A score of 5 means you are extremely well qualified to receive college credit, while a score of 1 means you are not qualified to receive college credit. While colleges and universities use scores differently, a score of 4-5 is equivalent to an A or B. A score of 3 is approximately similar to a C, while a score of 1-2 is comparable to a D or F. The examination is scored on a curve, adjusted for difficulty each year. In this way, your test score is equivalent to the same score achieved in different years.

Approximately 46% of students receive a 4 or 5 on the APUSH examination. Scores of 4 to 5 are widely accepted by colleges and universities; however, scores of 3 or lower may provide less credit - or none at all. More elite schools may require a score of 5 for credit and some schools vary the required score depending upon the department. You will need to review the AP policies at your college or university to better understand scoring requirements and credit policies.

While you'll take the APUSH exam in May, your scores will arrive in July. You can have your scores sent to the college of your choosing, or, if you're testing after your junior year, simply wait until you're ready to apply to the colleges of your choice.

Scoring on the multiple choice section of the examination is straightforward. You receive one point for each correct answer. There are no penalties for an incorrect answer or a skipped question. You should, if you're unsure, guess. Even a random guess provides you a one in four chance of scoring a point. If you can narrow down the choices just a bit, your chances increase and, along with them, your possible test score.

The Free Response Questions (FRQs) are scored from 1 – 8 depending upon the quality of the essay. Essay questions are graded by human graders, typically high school and college history instructors. They have been trained to grade the essays by the College Board. You'll find more information on FRQ scoring specifics later in the guide.

About This Guide

This guide will help you to master the most important test topics and also develop critical test-taking skills. We have built features into our books to prepare you for your tests and increase your score. Along with a detailed summary of the test's format, content, and scoring, we offer an in-depth overview of the content knowledge required to pass the test. In the review you'll find sidebars that provide interesting information, highlight key concepts, and review content so that you can solidify your understanding of the exam's concepts. You can also test your knowledge with sample questions throughout the text and practice questions that reflect the content and format of the APUSH. We're pleased you've chosen Accepted, Inc. to be a part of your journey!

PART I
Review

CHAPTER ONE

The Dawn of Colonialism
1491–1607

The years between 1491 and 1607 mark the first phase of European colonialism in North America. Prior to their arrival, Native Americans had varied cultures ranging from nomadic to urban, with seven geographic centers where populations shared cultural, architectural, agricultural, religious, and linguistic similarities.

Some Native American societies were extraordinarily large, and were organized around sophisticated political and philosophical concepts that predated Enlightenment ideas about representative government. In 1988, the Senate passed a resolution recognizing that the confederation of American colonies in the years leading up to the American Revolution was patterned on the pioneering governmental structure of the Iroquois Confederacy.

DID YOU KNOW?
Native Americans were significantly more advanced than they are typically represented in the popular media or high school history textbooks The Native American city of Cahokia, at its peak in 1250, had as many citizens as London and Venice.

The appearance of Europeans had a devastating impact on Native Americans. Within a few generations after contact, ninety-five percent of the North American native population died from a rampant plague: Eurasian smallpox, which European explorers unknowingly brought with them to the New World.

Before smallpox destroyed most of North America's native population, Giovanni da Verrazzano described the Eastern Seabord as "densely populated" and "so smoky with Indian bonfires" that you could smell it from hundreds of miles away. Yet, the misconception of pre-colonial North America as a vast, untouched, nearly empty wilderness—and the Native Americans as a primitive people—endures. This may be due to historians' overreliance on British colonial records, which were written by colonists who did indeed find a plague-ravaged, sparsely populated continent.

The Columbian Exchange

The Spanish and Portuguese established the COLUMBIAN EXCHANGE, which moved trade goods, animals and slaves between the Americas and "the old world," of Europe, Africa, and Asia. The exchange brought many changes to the Americas. Spanish horses dramatically altered trade and warfare, and Europeans traded technologies for valuable Native American goods.

The exchange also brought the plague that would kill some twenty million people in North America. Native Americans had no acquired immunity against Eurasian smallpox as the Europeans did, and lacked the knowledge to treat and contain the disease.

The slave trade, largely controlled by the Portuguese, was also part of the Columbian Exchange. West African slave merchants from the captured and enslaved people from the Gold Coast (which was in modern day Ghana, Nigeria, and Gabon) sold them to Europeans headed for the New World. Slaves worked sugar plantations, and later, cotton and tobacco plantations. Silver from the mines in South America helped to fund the slave trade.

The Spanish Colonies

There are many distinct differences between Spanish colonies and the Northern European colonies that would follow later in the sixteenth and seventeenth centuries. The most prominent difference may be the *ENCOMIENDA* SYSTEM, a Spanish forced-labor system that was fundamentally feudal in nature, and exploited and oppressed native peoples in the Americas and many other places around the world.

Later, European colonial demand for forced labor would far outpace fast-dwindling native populations ravaged by disease and oppression, so colonists in the Americas began importing African slaves through the Columbian Exchange.

While the Spanish used native peoples as slave labor, they also took native wives and mistresses, leading to a large number of *mestizos*, or individuals with mixed European and native blood.

THE TREATY OF TORDESILLAS granted the Spanish colonial rights to nearly all of the Americas, and a portion of Brazil to Portugal.

Spanish colonialism forms a key part of the history of this period, with lasting influences on the regional cultures of the southwest United States, California, and Texas.

Life in Europe

Colonialism impacted life in Europe significantly, both politically and demographically. Competition rose among European powers such as Spain, France, and Portugal to gain and control land and resources.

England did not establish a dedicated colonial presence in North America for much of the seventeenth century because it was racked with civil war and internal strife.

New foods, like corn and potatoes, helped to stabilize food supply, increasing the population and reducing the risk of famine. These also allowed for a larger part of the population to engage in non-food production-related activity, supporting movement toward MERCANTILISM, and later, CAPITALISM.

Banking systems grew, enabling traders to work more efficiently, and merchant groups rose in power alongside trade guilds of old. New forms of mercantile technology evolved to meet the needs of the booming New World trade. These included the sextant, a key navigation tool used by sailors, and the development of new, joint-stock companies to support colonial settlements and expeditions, particularly out of Britain. One example is the VIRGINIA TRADING COMPANY, which would establish and fund the Jamestown Colony in Virginia.

Changing Beliefs

Contact with new groups and cultures altered the worldviews and beliefs of people around the world. Most people had little awareness or understanding of individuals from different cultures until the dawn of the colonial era.

European attitudes toward native peoples (and later, Africans) were racist. Most considered non-European peoples to be inferior, but some Europeans considered native peoples fully human, while others thought of them as sub-human. The latter group's attitudes toward non-Europeans led to a pervasive, racist view of native people as a resource to be used and exploited.

The Spanish generally considered native people to be inferior, but fully human, and so undertook the conversion of many natives to Christianity. This was a high priority; some advocated teaching and preaching to native people in order to encourage their willing conversion; others promoted a policy of forced conversion. The philosopher Juan de Sepulveda identified native peoples as "natural slaves" and believed that forced labor was appropriate.

There was strenuous objection from some Europeans to the poor treatment of Native Americans, particularly from Jesuits like Bartolome de Las Casas, who wrote a treatise entitled *In Defense of the Indians*. Others, like Sepulveda, argued that Native Americans were "natural slaves" and advocated that they be forced to convert to Christianity.

Early Conflicts

: European desire to convert native peoples to Christianity, and to enslave them or rce them to live on European terms led to significant conflict. Native peoples rose up co defend their societies, beliefs, and cultural practices, and fought to maintain them in the face of overwhelming force and hardship.

This holds equally true for the Africans forced into slavery in the Americas. They worked to retain their own religious practices, language, and culture, frequently synthesizing them with local languages, beliefs, and culture. Escaped slaves formed "maroon societies," which aimed to retain many aspects of traditional African culture within these groups. In the modern world, some "maroon" religious syntheses can still be found, particularly in the South and the Caribbean – Vodun, or *voodoo*, is one example.

Europeans used various tools to encourage conversion. In some cases, conversions were voluntary, particularly where intermarriage occurred; in many others, they were forced. Spanish explorers and conquistadors founded towns throughout the Southwest, relying first on force to subdue native groups, then on religious missions and outposts to convert them. Missions provided food, shelter, and clothing in exchange for labor and compliance with European ideas about work, clothing and religion. Rebellion was relatively common, with many native people seeking to return to their previous way of life.

French attempts at religious and cultural conversion were small-scale and were not typically successful. Interactions between the French and native peoples in this period were most commonly trade-related. Relationships between the English and local native tribes varied. Early in the colonial period these were typically friendly, but limited, with minimal interaction or intermarriage. Later, as the English claimed more land, these relationships became more violent and volatile.

CHAPTER TWO
The New World
1607–1754

The period between 1607 and 1754 is marked by the conflict between native peoples and colonists in North America, as well as the development of new colonial and native cultures, impacted by the environment and interactions of different groups. While the beginning of the colonial era was marked by the clear dominance of the Spanish as a colonial power, diverse groups colonized North America in this period, with the Dutch, French, and British substantially increasing their land and colonial holdings. The Spanish retained control of portions of North America, including California and the Southwest. Each of these groups had their own colonization practices and actions. Slavery in North America grew substantially during this period, particularly in British-controlled areas.

THE SPANISH MISSION system grew significantly during this period. French and Dutch traders worked with native groups, particularly in the fur trades. These alliances were small in scale, involving a few individuals. Traders often married native women and maintained close, personal relationships with native groups. These traders typically had relatively limited relationships with other colonists.

DID YOU KNOW?
Between the mid-1600s and the mid-1700s, more than half of the people that arrived in New World colonies were slaves or indentured servants.

While the Spanish sought to control the natives and the French and Dutch maintained trade-based relationships, the English were the first to create large-scale agricultural colonies. Entire families moved to the English colonies with the goal of farming. Interactions with natives varied, but over time were progressively more hostile.

The Spanish tolerated and sometimes even encouraged intermarriage with locals and African slaves. While there were a large number of Spanish colonists, they were mostly young, single men. They had families in the colonies, and their children took on a relatively high social role.

The English, on the other hand, typically maintained few overt social interactions with native peoples, and frowned on intermarriage (with the notable exception of John Smith, the leader of Jamestown). This resulted in an insular society for English colonists. Since they moved their wives and families with them and generally avoided interactions with individuals of other races, they often found their settlements culturally and socially isolated, and did not benefit as much from positive relationships with local native populations as other colonial powers did.

The Rise of Slavery

A racial hierarchy developed in the English colonies of the Americas, which contributed to the rise of the institution of slavery. There were also several other key factors that ensured it would become a dominant practice in the new colonies:

▶ There was ample land for agricultural activity

▶ There was a lack of indentured servants

▶ British colonies failed to force native groups to labor

▶ Demand for colonial goods, like tobacco, was high

While slavery was established on tobacco and sugar plantations and elsewhere in the Americas from a very early date in the colonial era—Christopher Columbus himself enslaved most of the first natives he encountered in 1492—the practice grew widespread in the British colonies. The first African slaves arrived in the British colony of **Jamestown** in 1619. Initially, they were treated as indentured servants; however, the laws were soon changed to create the institution of lifelong chattel slavery, meaning that enslaved people received no pay and would never be set free.

Slaves were typically captured or kidnapped by West African traders and marched to coastal port cities. They were sold in chains and put in the lower cargo holds of ships. These ships travelled what is now called the **Middle Passage**, the route from Africa to the Americas, delivering slaves.

Between thirteen and twenty percent of slaves died during the journey, in which they lived in horrific conditions with little space, sanitation, health care, or even adequate food and water. Slave owners relied upon racial superiority to justify their actions. Racism also contributed to ongoing conflicts with native groups.

DID YOU KNOW?
In 1739, a slave revolt known as the Stono Rebellion (or Cato's Rebellion) resulted in 65 deaths. In response, the colonial government of South Carolina issued the Slave Code of 1740.

Africans resisted slavery in many ways. Though their families were often split by owners to discourage rebellion, African slaves still revolted violently on a frequent basis. When they could not, they worked to preserve their traditional African music, language, and culture in what ways were available to them.

In the British colonies, slavery continued to grow and along with it, the various moral and legal justifications for slavery also swelled. Racial divisions became progressively more intense throughout the English colonies. Amongst other groups, including the French and Spanish, racial divisions were much less clear-cut. In French-settled parts of modern Canada, the metis, or individuals born of mixed native and European marriage, played a significant role in society. In other French-settled and Spanish-settled lands, *mulattos*, or those born of African and European ancestry, could play a significant role—owning land and property—as could *mestizos*.

Jamestown

Jamestown was the first permanent English settlement in North America. Established in 1607 by the Virginia Trading Company, within three years, eighty percent of the colonists had died of disease, starvation, or battle with native tribes. Jamestown colonists also lacked the necessary skills to produce essential goods.

Through the skilled leadership of **John Smith**, a British admiral, the colonists built relationships with native tribes. Smith would go on to deed many plots of North American land to his colleagues, including William Penn, the founder of Pennsylvania.

Later, a colonist named John Rolfe introduced West Indies tobacco to Jamestown and went on to marry a Powhatan princess, **Pocahontas**.

The Puritans

The English colonies came to dominate the New World. They varied in personality, economic activity, and character depending upon the characteristics of the region, though the colonies of New England themselves lacked ethnic diversity. Founded and populated primarily by **Puritans**, they were both staunchly religious and dedicated to community-oriented life.

In 1630, the British ship *Arbella* landed at the **Massachusetts Bay Colony**, bringing many more settlers and, notably, the Puritan **John Winthrop**, whose famous sermon titled *A Model of Christian Charity* would become a seminal document in American culture. Winthrop, like other Puritans, believed the Bible was the source of all moral and legal authority, so there should be no separation of church and state.

Among many other tenets of their faith, Puritans also believed in **predestination**, the idea that human beings cannot escape fate. They also believed that society should be patriarchal (ruled by men) and that the most important things in life (in order) were:

1. God
2. Colony
3. Village

4. Congregation

5. Family

The land was fertile and the colonists engaged in both agriculture and commerce. The middle colonies were primarily grain-growing, with much of the grain intended for export to England. Further south, Chesapeake and North Carolina were primarily tobacco-growing regions, worked by indentured servants and enslaved people. The southernmost colonies, as well as those in the West Indies, produced a variety of goods for export, including cash crops like rice and sugar, as well as, at a later time, cotton. These regions had relatively small numbers of white colonists, but very large numbers of enslaved people from Africa or of African descent. These southern colonies enslaved the largest number of people, as they required massive amounts of physical labor.

In 1636, the **ANTINOMIAN CONTROVERSY** arose in the Massachusetts Bay Colony. The Antinomians, who were also known as Free Grace theologians, accused the Puritan leaders of preaching salvation that came through a "covenant of grace" with God, and not a "covenant of works." This was significant in that Antinomians were leveling the same charge at Puritans that Martin Luther, the father of Protestantism, leveled at the Roman Catholic Church with his famous Complaint. The Free Grace antinomians defied Puritan leaders with several acts of theological and political rebellion.

Notably, the antinomian **ANNE HUTCHINSON** began inviting groups of women—and as her fame grew, men as well—to gather in her home, discuss weekly sermons from Puritan clergy, and in some cases challenge them. This was a radical act for the time, as the early American colonies were highly patriarchal, excluding women from positions of power and responsibility, and demanding rigid obedience from them.

Though Anne Hutchinson did not take part in political demonstrations, she was arrested, imprisoned, and put on trial before both civil and religious authorities, including John Winthrop, who would go on to be the governor of Massachusetts. She was excommunicated from the church, and she fled from the Massachusetts Bay Colony. Later, when she and her family were indiscriminately slaughtered by native Siwanoy warriors at her home, John Winthrop said that the massacre "pleased the Lord."

Other British Colonies

A Puritan lay leader named Thomas Hooker organized a large group of colonists to form the **COLONY OF CONNECTICUT**, and in 1638 and 1639, he produced "The Fundamental Orders of Connecticut," which laid foundations for self-governance. This was the first written democratic constitution in recorded history.

In 1733, British General John Oglethorpe founded the colony of **SAVANNAH, GEORGIA.** He carefully planned the town to ensure its survival, and in an effort to attract settlers and provide a counterweight to the eminence of nearby Catholic Spanish colonies, he instituted religiously tolerant policies. Savannah became a diverse colony, attracting Lutherans from Germany, Huguenots from France, and Presbyterians from Scotland. The city became well-known for its openness to immigrants then, and throughout its history. Georgia officially became a Royal Colony in 1754, and the city of Savannah still stands today, unlike other early British colonies.

After several failed attempts at settlement, the **QUAKER** colony of Pennsylvania was founded in 1681 when John Smith deeded land to William Penn as payment for a debt. Over the next four decades, Penn led the colony and established the great American city of **PHILADELPHIA**.

Conflict and Competition

Spain, France, England, and the Netherlands competed politically and economically for American control. Trade alliances with native groups became highly valuable, both for wealth and to discourage warfare, and colonies frequently sought to preserve them and prevent other powers from creating similar alliances.

Perhaps the most significant conflict in the seventeenth century between Native Americans and colonists is now known as **KING PHILIP'S WAR**. In 1675, Metacom became Grand Sachem of the Wampanoag Confederacy, an alliance of native tribes. Metacom (also Metacomet or "King Philip" by the colonists) waged war against the British colonies for two years.

King Philip's War resulted in the destruction of twelve colonial towns and the deaths of almost 8,000 British colonists living in New England at the time. Metacom's campaign caused many of the colonies to band together and cooperate for defense and survival; the colonists defeated the Wampanoag Confederacy in 1676 at the Battle of Mount Hope. In this victory, the first glimmers of a cohesive American identity across different colonies could be seen.

This identity led the relatively independent colonies to become more politically and culturally similar. They shared similar laws, culture, values, and systems of government. This unification happened slowly, but as the colonists began to see themselves as distinct from England, the British Empire gradually responded by asserting more control over North American colonies. **THE DOMINION OF NEW ENGLAND** is a key example of this attempt to assert control. While Britain created the administrative dominion, the colonists objected, overthrowing the dominion within just a few years. Influenced by the **ENLIGHTENMENT** and religious movements like the evangelical Great Awakening, colonists began to rebel more and more against British control.

Other conflicts with Native Americans included the **Beaver Wars** and the **Chickasaw War**. The Beaver Wars, called the French and Iroquois Wars, occurred when Dutch and English colonists armed and supported the Iroquois in an uprising against the French in the mid-seventeenth century. The Chickasaw War of the eighteenth century illustrates the impact of conflicts between British and French colonists on native groups—the Chickasaw were supplied by and sided with the British against the French, who were allied with the Choctaw, and the two sides fought a bloody series of attacks and skirmishes that lasted almost two decades.

The colonies produced significant wealth for the parent country, directly (as with the silver mines of South America) and indirectly (like tobacco and furs). These goods were exported to Europe and sold. This led to the growth of export economies, as well as a growing need for control of land and economic resources, including, as noted above, alliances.

Mercantilism arouse in feudal Europe many years prior to the founding of the American colonies. Colonial goods made both European powers and the colonies wealthy; thus, power struggles ensued and the system led to significant historical developments. This would prove especially true for the American Revolution.

Growing Independence

Colonies typically had a state legislature with two houses and a governor. While property ownership was commonly required to vote, voting rights grew progressively over time. Women, slaves, and Native Americans were not allowed to vote, but eventually property ownership and voting taxes extended voting rights to poor and lower middle class white men.

Some of the most significant powers Royal Governors wielded included veto over assemblies, appointment and removal of officials, and the power to command militias. Though many royal governors sought the ability to print their own currency, they were never granted this right by colonial powers.

The goals and needs of colonists did not always mesh well with those of the parent country. This led to conflict that was often political rather than violent, over issues of taxation and defense.

For instance, in 1699, **the British Wool Act** limited the export of wool from the colonies. Wool could only be sold in the colony it was produced in. This Act was designed to support British wool production, but in doing so, it hurt colonial exports. **The Molasses Act** limited the import of molasses from the French West Indies, encouraging the import of molasses from British colonial properties. **THE NAVIGATION ACTS** limited the ability of colonists to sell goods to buyers outside of England, as well as the ships that could be used to transport goods. Additionally, these regulations and limits led to increased smuggling, as goods were transported and sold without government interference. Increased smuggling directly supported the growth of piracy.

Native Americans in the Colonial Period

Increased contact between Europeans and Native Americans led to more trading and more conflicts, especially as tribes acquired European gunpowder weapons. Europeans also supplied Native Americans with alcohol. As early as the seventeenth century, alcoholism became a prevalent and destructive force in Native American communities.

In this period, the Iroquois enlisted Dutch support to defeat the **HURON CONFEDERACY**, which was centered in the region north of the Great Lakes. These two Native American nations both supplied lucrative furs to European traders. European powers supported and sometimes engineered conflicts between Native American tribes and nations. In some cases, these conflicts had a long history, but access to European guns enabled new, bloody fights. The French, Dutch, and English settlers were all heavily involved in these activities, as were early corporations supporting trade between the Americas and Europe.

In New England, active efforts to convert Native Americans found some success. "Praying towns" or Christian communities of Native Americans, altered traditional gender roles and behavior among many tribes.

Atlantic Trade

The growth of American colonies led to a new trade network called the **ATLANTIC WORLD** that included Europe, the Americas, and Africa, and involved the exchange of goods, services, and people, both voluntarily and as slaves. Books also traveled across the Atlantic, spreading new ideas to America. Enlightenment thinkers like **JOHN LOCKE** supported the idea of natural rights to liberty, personal freedom, and a fair government, as well as religious tolerance.

In this time period, the British Parliament passed mercantilist policies called the Navigation Acts. The Navigation Acts stipulated that:

1. European goods going to colonies had to first pay duties at an English port.
2. Commerce to and from colonies could be carried only on English vessels.

3. Goods produced in the colonies, like tobacco, had to be shipped in certain quotas to England.

4. The transport of goods to the colonies from British ships and merchants was legally limited.

CHAPTER THREE
The American Revolution
1754–1800

By 1750, the white population in the British colonies totaled around two million people, divided almost evenly between the northern and southern colonies. Most of these colonies were near the coast, but settlers had begun to move inland. The southern colonies were predominantly made up of large-scale, plantation-style agriculture. In the north, cities were growing, but the Industrial Revolution had not yet begun. While slavery was legal in the north, it was relatively uncommon because there was relatively little need for significant agricultural labor.

As agrarian villages became towns, services such as shops and schools sprung up. In the south, towns served as trading centers, but the very wealthy lived on large plantations, worked by slaves. Wealthy southern families were not involved in the physical labor of farming, though most poor and middle-class individuals farmed, typically working small land holdings, without slaves. This does not mean that only rich Southerners advocated for slavery, however. The practice was so ingrained in the American consciousness—and the fear of violent slave uprisings was so deeply rooted—that poor and middle class Southerners stridently defended it as an institution, even if they did not benefit from it in a direct, material way.

For white American colonists, social mobility was a possibility in a way that was unthinkable in the rigid aristocratic hierarchies of the old world. An individual could move from the lower classes to the middle or even from the middle class to the upper. The sons of farmers and blacksmiths became administrators, businessmen, educators, and lawyers. Many of the **FOUNDING FATHERS** came from humble beginnings, themselves. **ALEXANDER HAMILTON,** the nation's first Secretary of the Treasury, was born out of wedlock to a single mother. **BENJAMIN FRANKLIN** was one of ten children born to a poor Boston family who couldn't afford to put him all the way through school, so he taught himself everything he needed to know to become a world-renowned author, scientist, statesman, diplomat, inventor…and the nation's first Postmaster General. America was a land of opportunity before the founding of the United States, and a meritocratic society based not on one's class at birth, but on one's natural talent and hard work, is still an ideal that many Americans consider their birthright and strive for today.

Unfortunately, social mobility for women, Native Americans, and free individuals of African origin was significantly more limited. There were few non-white individuals to gain real political power or prominence in pre-revolutionary America, and even fewer women of any race. Though women's political and individual agency was curtailed by colonial society, American women held significant cultural and social roles and enjoyed greater rights and freedom than British women.

The upper classes included wealthy merchants, government officials, clergy in the cities, and in the south, plantation owners. The middle class included most merchants and traders, skilled craftspeople, teachers, doctors, and small landowners. The lower class included those who did not own land, like tenant farmers, as well as free individuals of African origin, indentured servants, and apprentices. Enslaved people had no personal rights or freedoms and fell outside the tacit American class structure.

The French-Indian War

In 1754, the **FRENCH-INDIAN WAR** (also known as the North American theater of the Seven Years' War, which raged around the world) began. The primary parties in this war were French and British colonists, with economic and military support (including troops) from the European powers. Both sides recruited and armed local tribes of natives to fight for their side, but the French in particular depended on political and material trade with Native Americans, as they were outnumbered nearly thirty-to-one. Early in the war, the French allied with warriors from the Iroquois Confederacy in an attempt to wrest control of many territories in North America (mostly in French Canada) away from the British.

Early in the war, the French made significant gains, securing multiple victories against the British and their supporters and threatening the burgeoning American colonies. This was especially true in modern-day Canada, where French colonists living in Acadia (today's Nova Scotia and Canadian Maritimes) and their Native American allies waged an effective militia campaign of harassment against British supply lines.

The tide of the war turned between 1758 and 1760, when the British defeated France's Iroquois allies and gained control of Montreal. France ceded all of its territory east of the Mississippi River to British control, and its territory west of the Mississippi to Spain.

In 1763, the **TREATY OF PARIS** was signed, and King George III also issued the **ROYAL PROCLAMATION OF 1763**, guaranteeing unrestrained emigration for French colonists to leave newly conquered British territory.

This resulted in the **PROCLAMATION LINE OF 1763**, which deeded land west of the Appalachians to native tribes, and forbade colonists from expanding there. This caused significant rebellion in the colonies, causing some Native American groups, including the Iroquois Confederacy, to ally themselves with the British government against the colonies.

French colonists resettled across the continent; however, the culture of New France continues to live on today. In Montreal (in today's Canadian province of Quebec), French is still the official language, and is widely spoken. The modern-day state of Louisiana is home to New Orleans and the Cajun people, an ethnic group descended from the Acadians who maintain a French-influenced culture, including a unique spoken dialect of French.

DID YOU KNOW?
Both France and Britain suffered substantial economic harm as the result of this war, even though land gains put Britain in a position to consolidate its power in North America.

Continued Conflicts with Native Americans

With the end of the French-Indian War, Britain now controlled a significant part of North America. With lands under British control, the colonies continued to expand westward. This expansion led to growing conflict with Native American groups, as they were pushed from their traditional homelands further west, across the Appalachian Mountains. Some Native Americans, particularly those from the Great Lakes region, began to actively engage the colonists, attacking British forts. These attacks came to be known as the **PONTIAC WARS**.

In December 1763, on the Pennsylvania frontier, a group of Scots-Irish settlers calling themselves **THE PAXTON BOYS** banded together as a vigilante group and carried out attacks on a local Native American .group known as the Conestoga, a Susquehannock tribe that had peacefully coexisted with American colonists for decades. Claiming they had been attacked by the Conestoga, the Paxton boys killed several native people, including women and children, prompting the Pennsylvania government to place several at-risk Conestoga in protective custody. Despite being under the law's protection, the Paxton Boys broke in and killed six adults and eight children. In January 1764, the Paxton Boys marched to Philadelphia and met with Benjamin Franklin. Franklin perceived a threat in this band of vigilantes and worked fervently to convince them to disband. They agreed, in exchange for a public airing of their grievances against the Conestoga.

Though appalled at the Paxton Boys' deeds, Franklin kept his word and personally read their list of concerns to the state legislature. Both lawmakers and colonists resoundingly condemned the Paxton Boys, and Franklin later wrote that the Conestoga would have been "safe among any other people on earth, no matter how primitive, except the(se) white savages." The group never formed again.

Later, during the American Revolution, many Native Americans were loyal to—and fought for—the British, due to their alliance with the Crown, their hope to uphold the Proclamation of 1763, and the British provision of money, arms and other goods.

The Colonies Grow

The British territories in North America were experiencing some population shifts and changes during this period. Significant population increases were largely the result of a high birth rate. While voluntary migrants were still primarily English, there was a growing German population, totaling around six percent of the population, particularly in Pennsylvania. The term *Pennsylvania Dutch*, actually refers to German, rather than Dutch, immigrants. There were also a growing number of Scots-Irish immigrants, around seven percent of the population. These were individuals from the Scottish Lowlands who had been forced to move from Scotland to Ireland and then immigrated to the colonies. The Scots-Irish settled along the edges of the Appalachian Mountains. Approximately five percent of the population was made up of other European settlers, including French, Swiss, Welsh, and Scottish Highlanders. New England remained predominantly English, with lower colonies having a somewhat more diverse population. By the middle of the eighteenth century, around twenty percent of the American population was African, with the vast majority enslaved. Ninety percent of Africans lived in the southern colonies.

The Eve of Revolution

British victory over France created new conflicts that led to the **AMERICAN REVOLUTION**. The British had suffered significant losses, and increased financial demands on the colonies in response. Increased British mercantilist policies made life more difficult for the colonists.

In 1765, British Prime Minister Grenville imposed the **STAMP TAX**. The stamp tax required that a wide variety of forms of paperwork be stamped or printed on stamped paper. Payment for the stamps or stamped paper helped to fund the crown. For the British, this was a relatively common means of raising funds; however, the colonists did not see it favorably. The colonists questioned the legality of the Stamp Act, believing that only the colonial governments had the right to levy taxes, not Britain, because colonists had no representative seats in the British Parliament. The well-known slogan, *no taxation without representation* is the result of colonial protests of the Stamp Act. The Stamp Act was repealed in 1766.

The **TOWNSEND TEA TAX OF 1767** also triggered protests from the colonists. This was an import tax, rather than a direct tax; however, the colonists saw it as another British abuse. Loads of tea shipped to the colonies were taxed when they reached port. These taxes were designed to pay the salaries of colonial governors, but this did not reduce objections. By the time of the Townsend Tea Tax, approximately one million American colonists were regular tea drinkers, consuming the beverage at least twice each day. Tea smugglers became rich bringing the good into American ports, but they couldn't bring enough to satisfy demand, and soon the colonists rebelled, leading to British military intervention. While the British spent a substantial amount controlling protests in the colonies, the tax brought in little revenue.

The issue of taxation without representation—meaning that the British government levied revenue-raising taxes on trade without granting commensurate political power to the colonists—led to organized resistance efforts.

Local committees of correspondence were organized, first in Massachusetts, and later between the colonies. **SAMUEL ADAMS**, the cousin of future U.S.-president **JOHN ADAMS**, was integral in organizing the committees of correspondence, which played a key role in spreading information among the colonists. Though full-scale rebellion had not begun yet, a network had begun to grow. Yet, had history deviated just slightly from a perfect combination of events and circumstances, the American colonies might have had a very different future.

The Boston Tea Party

In 1773, the British gave the **EAST INDIA COMPANY** a monopoly on tea sales to the American colonies. The company was facing an excess in tea and could sell it very cheaply, but the colonists saw this as another overreach of British control. In New York and Philadelphia, protesters forced ships to turn back from the American ports.

In Boston, the authorities allowed East India Company ships into port, but a group of anti-British revolutionaries calling themselves the **SONS OF LIBERTY** snuck onto the ships (many dressed as Native Americans) and threw tons of cargo overboard in an act of protest against the trade monopoly.

In response, the British Parliament passed the four Coercive Acts in 1774. These came to be known as the **INTOLERABLE ACTS**:

1. The Boston Port Act closed the port of Boston until the city repaid all damages to the East India Company.

2. The Massachusetts Government Act revoked many of Massachusetts' legal rights, including self-governance.

3. The Administration of Justice Act gave British royal officials the ability to flee Massachusetts if they were accused of a crime and to have their

trial held elsewhere. Many colonists, including George Washington, felt this law would be abused by royal officials to act without regard to Massachusetts law.

4. The Quartering Act stipulated that British troops could be quartered within unoccupied buildings not otherwise designated for military use.

At the same time, Parliament passed the **QUEBEC ACT**, guaranteeing the citizens of Quebec a number of rights, including the right to practice Catholicism, retain the French language, and maintain some French legal customs. This alarmed citizens in the New England colonies, because it also repealed some British legal rights, such as the right to a trial by jury.

In response to the Intolerable Acts, the colonies summoned a **CONTINENTAL CONGRESS** to meet in Philadelphia in 1774. Twelve of the thirteen colonies sent their most distinguished and well-respected residents to the Congress.

This Continental Congress would meet many times over the coming years, in nine different cities, meaning that the United States has had nine different capital cities:

1. Philadelphia, Pennsylvania
2. Lancaster, Pennsylvania
3. York, Pennsylvania
4. Trenton, New Jersey
5. Princeton, New Jersey
6. Baltimore, Maryland
7. Annapolis, Maryland
8. New York City, New York
9. Washington, D.C.

The Continental Congress assembled a number of documents to present to the British Parliament, seeking additional rights for the colonies. These included a **DECLARATION OF RIGHTS** and the **APPROPRIATION**, a planned boycott of British goods until their demands were met, including an end to parliamentary taxation. Parliament refused their demands.

If the long, complicated relationship between the colonies and Britain had created a kind of political powder keg, the Boston Tea Party and the Intolerable Acts lit the fuse. The American Revolution was at hand.

The Shot Heard 'Round the World

The first acts of violence that marked the Revolutionary War began in April 1775. British troops, wearing their famous RED COATS, were deployed to Lexington and

Concord to seize colonists' supplies of gunpowder and to arrest Samuel Adams and **JOHN HANCOCK**, two leading revolutionaries. Warned in advance by **PAUL REVERE**, many American militiamen gathered for battle with the British. When the redcoats arrived in Lexington, they found close to 100 American fighters, known as **MINUTEMEN**, gathered in the town square. The British ordered them to disperse, but the Minutemen refused, leading to a tense standoff.

British officers ordered their men to hold their fire, and one British captain had even ordered his own men to disperse and go home when a shot was fired—most likely by a hidden gunman, whose loyalties are unknown to this day—resulting in an eruption of fire from the British regulars. The Minutemen were unable to resist the redcoats' attack, and several Americans were killed. In response, Minutemen from all over the colonies banded together to fight the British.

Britain had access to a large army, but lacked domestic support for its efforts to pacify the American colonies. There were relatively few loyalists on American soil, Britain was managing other struggles closer to home (including war with France) and King George III was not well-liked by the British public. Many British people were sympathetic to the colonists' grievances, even in the upper classes. Edmund Burke, a prominent lawmaker and political philosopher, regularly argued for conciliation with the American colonies on the floor of Parliament and openly expressed dismay at the Crown's actions, saying "I do not how to wish success to those whose victory is to separate from us a large and noble part of our Empire. Still less do I wish success to injustice, oppression and absurdity." As a result of the British public's ambivalence toward George III's policies, especially toward the colonies, British troops in America were often poorly supplied, and poorly managed.

America had a large number of willing volunteers, but limited access to adequate arms, uniforms, supplies, or training. They had fine leaders, including the **MARQUIS DE LAFAYETTE OF FRANCE** and a veteran officer of the French and Indian War, **GEORGE WASHINGTON**, to organize them. Benjamin Franklin, an inventor from Philadelphia, proved to have the diplomatic skills needed to secure foreign aid, particularly from France, to help the colonies meet their economic needs while resisting the British.

With the support of the Continental Congress in May 1775, the American colonies began to organize a revolution. They did not initially seek independence, but rather a successful British response to their petitions. With the support of the Continental Congress, George Washington was put at the head of the military response to Britain. Washington was a skilled leader, and as a wealthy Virginia planter with connections to both the northern and southern colonies, had the ability to unify Americans from across the new continent.

The Enlightenment and the Revolution

Had a number of ideological changes not occurred, the Revolutionary War may never have begun. Ideas from Enlightenment philosophers changed how the colonists thought about themselves, the government, and their interactions with one another. Eventually, these changes led to a true desire for independence, rather than cooperation with the colonial empire of Britain. These ideas were influenced by Enlightenment philosophy, which originated in Europe. The philosophers of the Enlightenment, including **JOHN LOCKE**, **MONTESQUIEU**, and **JEAN-JACQUES ROUSSEAU** supported the idea of natural rights like life, liberty, and the pursuit of happiness, as well as the idea that individuals and government work together, as the individual had to agree to be governed. The following concepts were key to the ideology of the American Revolution:

▶ **REPUBLICANISM:** an idea derived from the classical governments of Athens and Rome, republicanism was focused on the common good. Citizens supported the government and abided by laws set by the government because those laws supported the good of all within the state.

▶ **ANTI-AUTHORITARIANISM:** the colonists questioned the role of even a limited monarchy like Britain's. Anti-authoritarian forces advocated for a greater role for electoral bodies and are often associated with the Radical Whigs in the British government of this period. Electoral bodies were considered to be at less risk for corruption.

▶ **THE ROLE OF WOMEN:** women played a significant social role in this period. Some women, like Abigail Adams, were strong voices for the rights of women. Other women focused on education for girls and other efforts to improve women's lot. For the first time, the idea of "Republican motherhood" formed in American colonies.

In 1776, **THOMAS PAINE** published *COMMON SENSE*. This pamphlet, for the first time, called for true independence from Britain, rather than merely additional freedoms or improved relationships with the colonial power. Paine, in *Common Sense*, called for representative democracy, rather than aristocratic rule. While not all accepted his ideas immediately, they changed the goals of the revolution and the new American government. The Philadelphia Congress, after some argument, adopted the notion of independence, in full, in July 1776. The formal **DECLARATION OF INDEPENDENCE** was drafted by **THOMAS JEFFERSON** and approved by the Congress on July 4, 1776.

Following the Declaration of Independence, a revolutionary fever spread through the colonies. In New York, rioting broke out after George Washington read the Declaration of Independence in public, and colonists pulled down a large statue of George

DID YOU KNOW?

The Declaration of Independence was a letter to both the British Parliament and King George proclaiming the reasons that the colonies wanted to separate from Britain. In many ways, it was also a final effort to convince the British government to free the colonies for ideological reasons, and without going to war.

III, which was later melted down to make ammunition for American muskets. British loyalists were harshly treated, and some fled.

Most American colonists, however, favored the efforts of the American Revolution. There were no clear victors in the battles between the colonists and the British during the period between 1776 and 1778; however, the intervention of the French in 1778 changed the war dramatically. While the French were the first to ally themselves with the colonists, Spain and Holland soon also declared war against Britain and other European powers saw the opportunity to gain power, including Russia. In October 1781, the American colonists forced the surrender of General Cornwallis in Yorktown. While George III did not surrender at this time, the war was effectively won. In 1783, all parties agreed to the **PEACE OF PARIS**, officially granting America independence and ending the colonial relationship with Britain. The terms of the Peace of Paris included:

▶ The borders of the United States reached the Mississippi in the west, the Great Lakes in the north and Florida in the south.

▶ The Americans agreed not to prosecute loyalists, to allow British creditors to collect on their debts, and to return confiscated property to the loyalists.

Democratic Government

The American Revolution, as well as other revolutions elsewhere in the world, led to new ideas about democracy, which created new forms of government. These developed progressively, over time, but the ideals on which the new country of the United States of America became an example to people across the world. While the Declaration of Independence marks the first statement of American ideals and intentions with regard to government, it was far from the last.

A number of difficulties confronted the former colonies immediately. These included the **SEPARATION OF CHURCH AND STATE**, voting rights for those of lower socio-economic classes, slavery and emancipation, and changing ideas about social roles. This was a time of significant economic challenges, as the union of colonies had to find its way and develop its own industry without access to some forms of British trade. In order to resolve these issues and form a philosophical basis for a new American government, the Continental Congress asked each state to create its own constitution. These were, like the U.S. Constitution today, documents that defined the role of the government, including both rights and limitations. They were relatively similar to one another and all featured a strong legislative branch and much weaker executive and judicial branches. Each state was a sovereign entity. While they were willing to work together, they were not unified into a single nation at this time. The individual state constitutions helped to pave the way for an eventual federal constitution.

The Continental Congress drafted the Articles of Confederation in 1776. The Articles of Confederation provided the states with a framework of interconnectedness;

however, there were many problems. Designed to provide the French with guarantees of American unity, the Congress designed by the Articles of Confederation was weak, with few powers. Each state had a single vote in the Congress. The Congress could not raise taxes or compel the states to act. Ultimately, the Articles of Confederation did not address a number of difficult political problems, including an overall lack of unity, tariffs between states, and a lack of common currency. The independent states faced widespread difficulties. Internationally, Britain and Spain were both quite unfriendly to the colonies, and France demanded repayment of wartime loans. In some states, rebellion continued. In Massachusetts, **Shay's Rebellion** swung popular support behind the idea of a national army, rather than individual state militias.

The Constitution

In 1787, each of the states sent their best minds to Philadelphia to rewrite the Articles of Confederation. Only Rhode Island did not send delegates to this Constitutional Convention. Some well-known names from the Revolution, like George Washington, Benjamin Franklin, and James Madison attended; however, others were not in the country or chose not to. Thomas Jefferson was in France, and Patrick Henry refused to attend.

There was a diverse variety of attendants, from small farmers to large landowners, and from wealthy merchants to lawyers. Most were Christians from different denominations, though the majority were deists.

Almost at once, it was agreed that a new document was essential, rather than a revision of the Articles of Confederation. There were two competing plans: **The Virginia Plan** allocated representation in a bicameral legislature on the basis of population, giving larger states a greater voice in government. **The New Jersey Plan** held that equal representation in a unicameral, or one-house legislature, was fairer to smaller states with low populations.

The Great Compromise created the legislature we know today. The House of Representatives is allotted by population allotment, with delegates serving two years per term. In the Senate, two seats are allotted to every state regardless of population. Senators serve for six years per term.

The Three-Fifths Compromise held that slaves would count as three-fifths of one person when tallying population for representation. The new Constitution also created a strong Executive branch led by the President, who served not only as the leader of the country, but also as the leader of the federal military. The Constitution created the **Electoral College** out of the fear of the power of unchecked majorities. It is still in use, if rather controversial, today.

The Electoral College gave larger states a greater say in the outcome of presidential elections. Several measures directly reduced the power of the general population.

The Senate was not directly elected by the people, but by state legislatures, while the Electoral College had the power to elect the president. The President also had the right to appoint judges, and the Constitution created a strong federal judiciary.

Many of the founding fathers were opposed to slavery, but debate over its legality was fierce, and threatened some fragile alliances between states. The Constitutional Convention decided to suspend the importation of African slaves after 1807.

The abolitionist delegates agreed to pass the Act Prohibiting Importation of Slaves in 1807, as well as the **FUGITIVE SLAVE CLAUSE**, because they believed slavery would eventually die out. This was a concession to Southern delegates, especially those from South Carolina and Georgia.

There were progressive movements toward abolitionism at this time. **ABIGAIL ADAMS**, the wife of John Adams, is frequently remembered for her desire for women's rights; she was also a strong abolitionist who encouraged her husband in that direction. Some states also began to move toward abolitionism as early as 1780 when Pennsylvania passed an Act for the Gradual Abolition of Slavery. This act declared all children born in the state to be born free, prohibited the import of new slaves, and required the registration of all slaves. Children born to slaves were indentured servants until the age of 28. This method of abolition was later embraced by other states. During this period, slavery expanded in the south and became progressively less common in the north. This division became progressively more significant over the first half of the nineteenth century.

The Constitution still had to be ratified by all of the states. This posed significant problems. Common arguments against a federal Constitution included fears that the presidency was too powerful, that a federal government would subsume states' rights, that senators should not be elected by state legislatures, and that there was no Bill of Rights. It was agreed that once nine of the thirteen states had ratified the Constitution, it would become law in those nine states.

Politically, the nation was now divided into the **FEDERALISTS**, who supported a strong federal government, and the **ANTI-FEDERALISTS**, who were more focused on state and individual rights. Noted Federalists included Alexander Hamilton, John Jay, and James Madison, who wrote the Federalist Papers, a group of articles explaining how the new government would work to the American colonists. The anti-Federalists, including Samuel Adams, Patrick Henry, and many of the poorer colonists, were typically less educated and less wealthy than the Federalists.

Several states ratified the Constitution quickly, with Delaware the first to do so on December 7, 1787. In Massachusetts, it was ratified only after Federalists promised to add a Bill of Rights. By June 1788, nine states had ratified the Constitution. The remaining four states followed.

DID YOU KNOW?
While you are likely familiar with material on the text of the Constitution and the Bill of Rights, if you feel a need for additional review, please see "Chapter 10: Reference Materials and Resources" for the full text of these historical documents.

George Washington took office with the unanimous support of the Electoral College on April 30, 1789. **THE BILL OF RIGHTS** was formally added to the U.S. Constitution in 1791.

The American Revolution and the charters set forth by the new government had lasting political repercussions for Haiti, France, several countries in Latin America and many more around the world, all of whom modeled their own democratic governments on American ideals.

The Growth of a Nation

In fewer than fifteen years, America declared its independence, fought a war for its freedom, and produced first the Articles of Confederation, and later, the Constitution and Bill of Rights. This was not without struggle—and there were more to come.

The young country also faced foreign policy problems, including a lack of control over foreign commerce, no provisions to protect settlers from Native Americans, little trade with Britain, and no provisions to repay France for loans made during the Revolutionary War.

There were also economic challenges. As president, Washington chose a close friend and colleague, Alexander Hamilton, to be the first secretary of the new national treasury. The son of a single mother and a former shopkeeper, Hamilton was a "self-made man." He instituted a national currency, worked with Thomas Jefferson to assume individual state debts as federal, issued securities to pay off the debts, and created a **NATIONAL BANK**. He adopted mercantilist policies to support the growth of the American economy and encourage American manufacturing, rather than see the nation rely on imported goods. This provided the basis for a strong and growing American economy.

Hamilton also drafted the **JAY TREATY**, negotiated by John Jay, which led to a successful and beneficial trade relationship with Britain. This also brought an end to the tensions with the British that remained after the Revolution. While this treaty had a number of economic consequences, it also included the withdrawal of British forces from the Northwest Territory.

DID YOU KNOW?
Hamilton and Thomas Jefferson were philosophically opposed on a number of issues, and fought bitterly during their time in George Washington's cabinet.

America also now had to play a role in the global community. While close alliances with France had been essential for American success in the Revolutionary War, when Revolutionary France declared war against Britain, and eventually, the remainder of Europe in 1793, America opted to formally proclaim its neutrality, rather than becoming involved in the war. Jefferson, who supported neutrality, nevertheless became embroiled in a political scandal involving a French minister, known as Citizen Genet, attempting to recruit Americans to fight for the French. After Washington expelled Genet from the United States, Jefferson resigned.

Despite his resignation, Thomas Jefferson's political influence in the new country could hardly have been greater. The first political parties developed in the 1790s, largely split between Jefferson's followers, who called themselves Democrat-Republicans and were more supportive of individual state's rights, and the Federalists, who were more closely associated with Alexander Hamilton's views on a strong federal government and isolationist foreign policies.

The Federalists and the Democratic-Republicans remained the two dominant political parties in the United States until the 1830s. In broad terms, the Federalists represented the interest of wealthy land owners, while the Democratic-Republicans appealed more strongly to the middle classes, as well as the interests and needs of this group.

Westward Migration

While the Revolutionary War and changing government are key features of this period, it is not the only important historical consideration. With the final settlement of the Revolutionary War, the United States gained lands as far west as the Mississippi River. This marked the beginning of huge westward expansion for the new American nation— and the end of sovereignty and freedom for many Native American tribes.

In 1780, the **NORTHWEST ORDINANCE** allowed for new and increased settlement in the west, providing a method for new territories to be added to the United States. As settlers moved west, their need to navigate the Mississippi River increased. The Mississippi, as well as the American Southwest, were still under the control of Spain. This led to increased diplomatic contact with Spain, as the United States sought rights to the river. Pinckney's Treaty in 1796 solidified and clarified relations between Spain and the United States. The treaty allowed the United States. to navigate the Mississippi River and clarified the boundaries between the United States and Spanish-controlled territories to the west. The United States also gained some trade privileges with Spain and the right to move cargo within the harbor of New Orleans, which was still under Spanish control during this period.

In the west and southwest, Spanish missions grew, particularly in California. Mission architecture was simple and consistent, relying upon locally available materials and building techniques. The mission included not only a church and housing for the priests, but also space for soldiers and servants, workshops, and storage rooms. Spain had worked hard to convert many Native Americans to Christianity, while still allowing many traditional religious and cultural customs and practices. As in other Spanish settlements, there was more cultural blending than in the United States at this time. As a result, a number of new traditions developed in these regions. Some Native Americans became skilled cowboys, or *vaqueros*, working with livestock on large tracts of land. The roping and animal husbandry skills they developed remain a part of western American tradition today. The *corrido* also developed, which are story-songs or ballads, sang or chanted depending upon the region and tradition.

New Conflicts

At the **1783 TREATY OF PARIS**, Britain revoked the Proclamation of 1763 and handed the Native American lands west of the Appalachians over to the new United States. Because Native Americans were not represented at that meeting, they did not legally recognize the Treaty of Paris, and actively resisted expansion into their lands. This led to violent conflicts between white settlers and natives as Native Americans fought to keep sovereignty over their existing land, and American settlers pushed them ever westward.

Most significantly, the **NORTHWEST INDIAN WAR** involved the United States and the Western Confederacy—a united group of native tribes including the Shawnee and the Mohawk. The conflict began in 1785 in the Northwest Territory, located between the Ohio River, the Great Lakes, and the Mississippi River as a series of skirmishes and raids between white settlers and native militias. In 1790, George Washington sent in the U.S. Army—then a fairly ragtag, poorly equipped fighting force—to assert American sovereignty over the region. The U.S. Army was roundly defeated in a number of battles by the Western Confederacy over the course of two years. When General Anthony Wayne took command, the United States began winning tactical and strategic victories against native fighters across the Northwest Territory. The U.S. Army eventually defeated the Western Confederacy in the **BATTLE OF FALLEN TIMBERS** in August 1794.

Shortly thereafter, in 1796, two European powers—Britain and Spain—would begin actively working to consolidate colonial power in North America despite the presence of the new United States. This would lead to future conflicts and resultant developments in America's role in world politics.

CHAPTER FOUR
Exploration and Innovation
1800–1848

When Thomas Jefferson decided to seek the Presidency in 1800, he found an unlikely ally in his old rival, Alexander Hamilton.

Hamilton was a Federalist and Jefferson was a Democratic-Republican, yet despite their philosophical and political disagreements on many crucial issues of the day, Hamilton went against his own party's candidate, John Adams, and actively campaigned for Jefferson. Later, the second U.S. Vice President, Aaron Burr, would kill Hamilton in a duel.

Though Hamilton never served as president of the United States, as the first Secretary of Treasury and a Founding Father, he nevertheless appears on the $10 bill.

Jefferson's presidency was monumentally important to the new United States. Among his accomplishments in the White House, Jefferson doubled the size of the United States by making the **LOUISIANA PURCHASE** from France, sent **LEWIS AND CLARK** to explore the Pacific Northwest, and reduced the young nation's crippling debt by 25%.

Jefferson also repealed the **ALIEN AND SEDITION ACTS**, passed by John Adams, which were a group of laws that suppressed non-Federalist voters.

Just before he left office, Jefferson passed the **NON-INTERCOURSE ACT OF 1809**, which prevented U.S. ships from trading with Britain and France. The resultant tensions were one of the direct causes of the War of 1812.

The Era of Good Feelings

Europe was at war at the beginning of the nineteenth century, as Napoleon's armies methodically conquered the continent for the French Empire. This affected U.S. trade with Europe at first, but soon became a foreign policy crisis, as both the British and

French attempted to seize American commercial ships, and the British captured and forced thousands of American sailors into the service of the British Navy. In 1807, a British ship attacked an American vessel just off the U.S. coast, a provocative act that incensed the American public. Rather than go to war, President Thomas Jefferson responded by passing the **EMBARGO ACT OF 1807**, with the goal of pressuring Britain and France to respect American neutrality. However, the act backfired; the primary source of funds for the U.S. government was tariffs, or fees and taxes, imposed upon imported goods. Since many imports came from Europe, the Embargo Act immediately slashed revenue from tariffs and wreaked havoc on the American economy. This led to significant civil unrest in the United States, particularly in merchant-heavy New England. It was repealed fifteen months later, in 1809.

Despite Jefferson's blunder in the first decade of the 19th century, his political party was ascendant. After the end of America's involvement in the War of 1812, and the end of the Napoleonic Wars in Europe, a period known as the **ERA OF GOOD FEELINGS** began in 1816, with James Monroe's landslide election to the presidency over his Federalist opponent. A Federalist was never again elected to the presidency, and soon thereafter, the political party ceased to exist.

DID YOU KNOW?
The Era of Good Feelings was a time of growing nationalism in America, spurred on by Monroe's goodwill tour around the nation. However, not all of the nation was feeling good—there was intense political conflict over internal issues including tariffs, the national bank, and slavery.

In the south, support for slavery was growing in several ways. Large-scale landowners relied upon slaves to work their land; however, support for slavery extended far beyond the wealthiest classes. The institution of slavery allowed lower-class whites to work their own land, since the need for labor was filled by slavery. This created a lower class of land owners with small holdings or farms of their own. Therefore, slavery benefited both the upper and lower classes, although in different ways. Slavery and the support for slavery became progressively more important to the southern identity, and this began the rift between the South and the rest of the nation.

In 1819, the United States experienced a significant economic recession precipitated by a financial crisis, now known as the **PANIC OF 1819**, which was driven by strong speculative investment in the west, including investments by the national bank. The Panic of 1819 led to widespread bullying of western banks (called "wildcat" banks) and the national bank foreclosed on many private mortgages around the nation, but particularly in the West. This emphasized the divisions between the wealthy and upper middle classes and working classes, because those who could not pay their debt were often sent to prison—sometimes over just a few dollars. The states took the lead in passing legislation to close these prisons, though the federal government itself would not outlaw the practice until 1833, and the last debtor's prison didn't close until 1849.

The Monroe Doctrine laid out U.S. foreign policy during this period. With the support of Britain, the Monroe Doctrine set out a plan to prevent further European colonization of the Americas, protect the United States from a strong anti-democratic movement that was building in Europe and potentially looking across the Atlantic, and a promise to protect the independence of Latin American countries. This policy echoed George Washington's belief that America should remain uninvolved in the affairs of the world, but was eventually used to support both American isolationism and expansionism.

The Supreme Court also began to define federal powers more clearly, placing federal law above state law, under Chief John Marshall (sometimes called The Last Federalist.) Some of his key decisions include:

▶ *McCullough v. Maryland* in 1819 established the rights of the federal government to create a federal bank, the Second Bank of the United States. The state of Maryland had attempted to tax all bank transactions at any bank not chartered in the state of Maryland. The court's support of the federal government in this instance clarified the "necessary and proper" clause of the U.S. Constitution, expanding the powers of the federal government, and deemed the state tax on the bank in Maryland to be unconstitutional.

▶ *Worcester v. Georgia* clarified the rights of the federal government and states with regard to Native American land. In this case, decided in 1832, the state of Georgia had made it illegal for any non-Native American to be on Native American land without a license from the state. This was a criminal conviction. The *Worcester v. Georgia* decision determined that Native American land was to be treated as Indian nations, with relations handled between nations, or between the federal government and the Indian nation. This decision determined that the states had no rights with regard to relations with Native Americans and no rights over Native American land.

▶ *Cohens v. Virginia* established the federal Supreme Court's ability to review state-level Supreme Court decisions involving the powers of the federal government

▶ *Fletcher v. Peck* established landmark property rights and the responsibility of states to uphold their contracts to private organizations

In 1824, all four candidates in the presidential election that year identified as Republicans. After one candidate withdrew from the election due to illness, Henry Clay threw his support behind New Englander John Quincy Adams for the presidency in a move commonly called the **Corrupt Bargain of 1824** because Adams appointed Clay to the position of Secretary of State upon election. The remaining candidate, Andrew Jackson, responded with significant anger to this bargain.

DID YOU KNOW?
Between 1800 and 1828, the Democratic-Republican Party (then widely called the Republican Party, or Jefferson's Republicans) controlled the White House and dominated American politics.

John Quincy Adams' presidency was unpopular, as he entered the presidency under charges that he had corruptly "traded" the office of Secretary of State for Clay's electoral support. Adams, despite being the son of the nation's second president, was also not well-suited to politics. **Andrew Jackson,** commonly called "Old Hickory," won a landslide victory over him in 1828, and threw open the doors of the White House to all Americans. Upon his election, the nation entered an even more pronounced era of anti-Federalism focused on egalitarianism, states' rights and sectionalism, and the Democratic-Republican Party split into two factions—**DEMOCRATS**, who were loyal to Jackson, and **WHIGS**, whom were loyal to Henry Clay. Though there were other minor parties, the Democrats and Whigs would soon become the dominant two parties in America.

DID YOU KNOW?
Sectionalism is significant or excessive concern for local issues, with little interest in broader national politics.

Cultural Change

The ideology of the Enlightenment grew and changed during the first half of the nineteenth century. New ideas appeared, building upon the basic philosophy that had helped to shape the Declaration of Independence, Constitution, and Bill of Rights.

The first inklings of social change appeared in this period, commonly called the **SECOND GREAT AWAKENING**. These were primarily driven by religious and social organizations that helped to foster growing political interest in women's rights, abolitionism, and utopianism. Many of these organizations were primarily composed of well-off or upper middle class women and were frequently closely connected to religious movements.

CHARLES GRANDISON FINNEY is one of the fathers of the Second Great Awakening. A Christian Evangelist, Finney was an outspoken abolitionist and supporter of women's rights. He believed in and preached the doctrine of Christian Perfectionism. The doctrine of Christian Perfectionism believed that the heart of a born-again or saved Christian would be free of original sin and full of love for both God and others. This was a strong overall belief in the role of grace in salvation, and a condemnation of the Calvinist idea of pre-destination. Members of Finney's organization were actively involved in a variety of causes and movements, including the **UNDERGROUND RAILROAD**, helping to move slaves to freedom. As President of Oberlin College in Ohio, Finney accepted both African-American and female students, creating the first integrated campus.

In 1848, the first convention on women's rights, the **SENECA FALLS CONVENTION**, took place in Seneca Falls, New York. This convention is often used to mark the beginning of the women's rights movement in the United States.

Well-known names in the fight for women's rights and suffrage, or the right to vote, include **LUCRETIA MOTT** and **ELIZABETH CADY STANTON**. Other issues on the agenda for women included the right to own property (particularly after marriage), serve on juries, and receive fair pay for their work. The women's rights movement was strongly supported by the Quaker Society, particularly common in Pennsylvania, as well as abolitionists, including Frederick Douglass. The women's rights movement also played a key role in early labor rights movements, including the desire for a five-day work week, rather than a six-day work week. Some of these women, like Lydia Maria Child, worked for the rights of all subjugated groups, including women, Native Americans, and African-Americans. Eventually, the division between those who supported only women's rights and those who spoke out broadly for various social concerns and considerations divided the women's rights movement.

The first Utopian communities also appeared during this period. These were planned and designed communities, typically relatively small, and organized around a specific philosophy, often religious, but not always. In many cases, property was held in common. Some communities thrived for a time, while others were quite short-lived. Typically, the more restrictive the community the less likely it was to last. Some communities experimented with unusual forms of marriage or social behavior, like the Oneida colony, which considered all members married to one another. The Shakers were one of the longest-lasting and most stable of these Utopian experiments, which took their name from Thomas Moore's Renaissance-era book of the same name.

In the North, the **ABOLITIONIST MOVEMENT** grew. The importation of slaves stopped, as required by the Constitution, in 1807. However, the institution of slavery continued. Many Northern states had already embraced abolition, implementing both long- and short-term means of emancipating slaves in their states. While there were a growing number of free African-Americans, particularly in the northern states, they lacked many basic rights or protections. The Abolitionist movement included a number of smaller movements, as well.

The **AMERICAN COLONIZATION SOCIETY** or ACS sought to help return former slaves and free African-Americans to Africa. The organization, established in 1817, helped found the country of Liberia in West Africa during the Monroe presidency (the capital of Liberia today is named Monrovia in his honor.) The ACS had the support of both abolitionists and slaveholders. Slaveholders objected to abolition, but saw the repatriation of freed slaves and free African-Americans as a possible solution, while abolitionists, including the Quakers, saw this as a benevolent movement to help freed slaves. The ACS remains controversial among scholars today as to whether the organization was, at its core, racist, or a well-intentioned attempt to atone for the American sin of slavery.

Most students in AP U.S. History are already familiar with the Underground Railroad; however, you should remember that most of those involved were everyday people, working to help others because they felt it was the right and moral choice. The Underground Railroad began during this period, but was at its height between 1850 and 1860.

In 1845, Frederick Douglass published his autobiography, *Narrative of the Life of Frederick Douglass, an American Slave*. He was already a noted speaker and orator, and well-known in abolitionist circles. His work brought additional attention to the plight of the slaves, and brought into question the southern justifications for slavery. Often, those who supported slavery portrayed the

DID YOU KNOW?
The Underground Railroad moved escaped slaves from the south to the north, where they could be free.

slaves as sub-human, lacking the ability to reason, and unable to be educated. Douglass' writing and speeches proved all of those claims to be untrue.

The many social movements in the first half of the nineteenth century spawned reactionary responses. As the ethnic makeup of the United States changed, XENOPHO-BIA increased. Racism was common in the north, limiting the options of free African-Americans, while pro-slavery movements remained strong in the south. Policies limiting the land and rights of Native Americans also increased, further marginalizing the native population.

Social movements were of great importance, but America also began to define its own artistic, religious, literary, and architectural styles. Various religious sects thrived as religion became more diverse. Some of these were immigrant groups, like the Amish. Other groups also created distinct cultures, including many Native American groups, women, and a growing middle class. Native American groups merged, changed, and evolved as they moved progressively westward. For some tribes, horses became progressively more important.

The middle class, educated, employed, and with some amount of wealth, found their own identity, separate from both those who worked the land and those who held substantial wealth; however, this too was changing. Industrialization brought a new level of social mobility, allowing some members of the middle class to attain wealth. Each of these made up only one small part of a developing American culture.

In the visual arts, a new interest in landscape painting appeared in both Europe and the United States. In America, the Hudson River School painted scenes of the Hudson River Valley and surrounding area, including the Adirondack Mountains. THOMAS COLE is the founder of the Hudson River School, becoming well-known beginning in 1825.

You may already be familiar with another well-known artist of this period, JOHN JAMES AUDUBON. Audubon was a naturalist and a painter, particularly of birds. *The Birds of America* dates to the 1820s and 1830s and remains a fine work in the field of ornithology, the study of birds.

In architecture, the Federal Style developed, uniquely American. The Federal Style was neoclassical, with large windows, white walls, and some decorative elements. The early buildings in Washington D.C. are all an example of the Federal Style, as is Thomas Jefferson's home, Monticello.

African-American culture also grew and developed during this period. In many ways, cultural traditions evolved to help preserve traditions, families, and customs, particularly in the south. In the north, some free African-Americans, like Frederick Douglass and other abolitionists, played a growing social and political role. Douglass was not the only well-known African-American abolitionist. In Massachusetts, DAVID WALKER called for an active fight against slavery and inequality in his 1829 APPEAL IN FOUR ARTICLES. Walker is particularly of note because he called for not only abolition, but challenged notions of inequality and racial unfairness. RICHARD ALLEN, the founder of the African Methodist Episcopal Church founded a church designed to meet the needs of both free African-Americans and those recently escaped from slavery. Allen was born a slave, but became a prominent voice for freedom and education within his community, both in Philadelphia and beyond. His second wife, SARAH ALLEN, a former slave, is remembered as the founding mother of the AME church. While these movements were directly political, slaves also found ways to create and retain culture.

One of the best-known and most important of these is slave music. There were three distinct types of slave songs. The first is religious, with some well-known hymns common in African-American churches developing during this period. Work songs were sung during work to help pass the time, and allow individuals to maintain a rhythm in their work. Finally, recreational songs brought happiness and joy into their lives, typically sung along with string instruments.

One notable Native American from this time period was named SEQUOYAH, who was from the Cherokee tribe. Sequoyah invented the Cherokee alphabet, allowing reading and writing in that language for the first time in history; after the Cherokee Nation officially adopted it, their literacy rate soared to levels much higher than any other surrounding white or Native American settlements. Sequoyah's statue can be found in the U.S. Capitol building today.

The Industrial Revolution

The **INDUSTRIAL REVOLUTION** began in Britain in the second half of the eighteenth century. By the beginning of the nineteenth century, it had spread from Britain to America. The Industrial Revolution impacted all forms of production, including agriculture and manufacturing. It was accompanied by a growth in new technology directed toward transportation, manufacturing, industry, and agriculture. The first technological innovations of the Industrial Revolution were related to textile production, moving the former cottage industry into large-scale factories. This technology was brought from Britain to the United States by **SAMUEL SLATER**.

Slater opened the first American textile mills, including Slater Mill in Rhode Island, creating company villages that employed the entire family, including children. These villages included housing, stores, and Sunday school programs to teach reading and writing. Eventually, Slater also acquired the ability to produce iron, enabling him to build his own machinery.

Two significant agricultural innovations in the United States were the steel plow and the mechanical reaper. The STEEL PLOW was invented by John Deere in 1837. As settlers moved into the Midwest, they were unable to plow the hard soil there with the traditional wooden plows. The steel plow was invented to work the harder and more challenging soils of the Midwest. The

DID YOU KNOW?
Other significant innovations of the Industrial Revolution included the telegraph, the steam engine, the railway, and mass production.

MECHANICAL REAPER was a practical and productive way to harvest grain. Prior to the 1830s, all grain was reaped by hand, with a scythe. The mechanical reaper was pulled by horses, cutting the grain as it moved through the fields. There is some dispute over the inventor of the mechanical reaper, as two men invented reapers, independent of one another within a few years of each another. While Cyrus McCormick is often credited with the invention, Obed Hussey invented a reaper before McCormick and the McCormick reaper did not become successful until McCormick acquired rights to Hussey's cutting blade.

With the advent of industrialization, life in America changed. People moved from the countryside to the cities or to company towns. Rather than working at small farms, more people, including women and children, were employed in factories. These were, by and large, unskilled workers and were paid poorly. There were no labor laws providing any form of protection during this period. Eventually poor labor conditions led to the formation of the first labor unions, created to allow workers to advocate for improved work conditions. Workers did not have the legal right to unionize, but began organizing around the middle of the nineteenth century. The first unions did not appear until 1866.

Slater instituted the idea of company towns; however, this advanced and expanded in the LOWELL SYSTEM. While Slater's mills were spinning factories, the weaving was sent out. The entire family lived in the company town and often worked in the mill. In the Lowell System, all forms of textile production took place in the factory, including spinning the thread, weaving the cloth, dyeing, and cutting the fabric. These companies did not employ the entire family, but only young women. The workers were unskilled, typically from rural communities, and lived in company-run boarding houses. Their lives were tightly regimented, with an 80-hour work week and strict regulations on their behavior. The Lowell System declined around the end of this period, ending completely with the Civil War, and Irish immigrants began to work in the textile mills.

The Baldwin Locomotive Works built the first trains in the United States. Matthias Baldwin, who originally produced steam engines, first built a miniature locomotive before going into business as a full-size locomotive manufacturer. The first locomotive engine, OLD IRONSIDES, was built in 1832 and followed by many more, with some variances in production depending upon the economy.

The Industrial Revolution also required fuel for its steam engines, steam ships, and locomotives. Coal was the primary source of power for all of these. Large quantities of coal required larger and more developed coal mines. The first significant large-scale anthracite coal mining operation began in northern Pennsylvania with the Lehigh Coal Mining Company. They shipped the first load of coal from their mines in 1820. Coal fueled all parts of the Industrial Revolution, taking the place of water power and providing a more efficient means of production.

The Industrial Revolution increased the regional separation within the United States, with changes occurring in both the North and the South:

- ▶ Raw materials, particularly cotton, were produced in the South. These were shipped to the North and produced into goods for sale or export. Cotton production fueled the slave trade at this time.

- ▶ Finished goods were produced in the North, including textiles, locomotives, and iron.

- ▶ Agricultural goods were produced in the Midwest and sold to the North; however, the Midwest and North were relatively closely interconnected.

These economic shifts impacted population and migration. The South relied on its exports in order to survive, but experienced no significant immigration. The North and West experienced significant migration, as communities of newcomers arrived to fill the growing number of industrial jobs available. Their moves to the west offered new opportunities for immigrants new to the country. These changing populations created new, close-knit communities. Some communities were connected by ethnicity, as immigrants moved to join others from their own country. In these ethnic enclaves, they could speak their own language, help one another find housing and work, and start new lives. Others were connected by simple location. As settlers moved further west, they had to form their own communities and support one another in order to survive.

The Industrial Revolution also changed the role and understanding of social classes in America. While the onset of industrialization led to a greater divide between rich and poor, it also created a new working class. These individuals were not poor, but were also not rich. For the first time, work and home were different and distinct. Prior to the Industrial Revolution, most working or tradespeople lived and worked in the same location. Often, all members of the family of working age worked in the family business. They interacted on a consistent, daily basis, with all members engaged in business activity. This changed as work and home became two separate locations. This change altered family and home life in a number of different ways, particularly for women.

Earlier in this unit, we discussed the growing women's rights movement; however, this existed alongside a particular definition of and expectation of women, particularly white, American-born, upper-class women. Called the CULT OF DOMESTICITY or the CULT OF TRUE WOMANHOOD, this expectation did not apply to women of the lower classes, immigrant women, or African-American women. Women were expected to be submissive, pious, pure, and domestic. The home, husband, and children were to be their sole focus, without any significant distraction from their domestic work. It was acceptable to engage in charitable affairs, particularly those impacting socially-appropriate causes, but women were not encouraged to read, learn, study, or work. While the Cult of Domesticity did not necessarily apply to women of all classes, over time, the number of working married women declined dramatically and many women were forced to leave the workforce if they married.

Manifest Destiny

The Treaty of Paris provided the United States with substantial land, while later treaties with Spain gave the country the right to navigate the Mississippi. The Louisiana Purchase in 1803, during the presidency of Thomas Jefferson, dramatically expanded the western territories of the United States, opening up new land for settlement. The United States was on the move, and growing larger, even if the Constitution did not specifically approve the purchase of new land. The Louisiana Purchase provided the United States with not only Louisiana, but land encompassing fifteen current U.S. states in part or total. The land extended north, beyond what is today the Canadian border. The Louisiana Purchase was only one step in an overall expansionist policy in the United States in the first half of the nineteenth century.

While the Louisiana Purchase marks the beginning of expansionism, it is only the beginning. Some other examples of American expansionism include:

▶ The **TREATY OF WANGHIA**, ratified during President John Tyler's term in 1844, provided for favorable trade relations between China and the United States. The United States gained the right to buy land in Chinese port cities, learn the Chinese language, build churches and schools, and set tariffs in Chinese ports.

▶ With a new level of diplomatic power, the United States could negotiate on a relatively equal basis with European powers, including Britain. The **WEBSTER-ASHBURTON TREATY OF 1842** negotiated the northern border of the United States and Canada, the use of the Great Lakes, and brought a final and lasting end to the international slave trade.

▶ The **OREGON DISPUTE** was a series of diplomatic negotiations between the U.S. government and the government of Great Britain over the border of what was then called Oregon Country. Eventually, Britain and the United States came to terms, settling on the forty-ninth parallel as the territorial border. The United States believed it had the right to land to the fiftieth parallel; however, neither country was willing to go to war.

▶ The United States embraced a belief in Manifest Destiny by the middle of the nineteenth century—the idea that it was the destiny of American settlers to expand all across the North American continent, and that it was not just a political imperative to do so, but a moral one. Manifest Destiny also encompassed a belief in the unique virtue of America, and played a key role in the election of 1844, which gave John Tyler the presidency.

▶ In 1845, the United States annexed the **REPUBLIC OF TEXAS**. While many citizens of Texas supported the annexation, the U.S. political parties did not. Texas was a slave-owning Republic at the time of the annexation, causing additional conflict. President John Tyler pursued annexation regardless of political support. In 1844, James Polk ran on a platform of Manifest

Destiny, supporting the annexation, which was passed by a Democratic legislature at the end of 1844.

While these were expansionist policies designed to enlarge the country, there was also a new desire to build broader trade relationships and engage in a variety of foreign policies designed to improve American economic and political power. While America was willing to engage economically and stated a willingness to defend itself and to support growing independence in Latin America, it also avoided active engagement in military or political activity elsewhere. As a growing power, the United States had the ability to act diplomatically, rather than through force.

Expansionism and the Native Americans

The Monroe Doctrine, Webster-Ashburton Treaty, annexation of Texas, and Oregon Dispute all illustrated the growing power of the United States and dominance over not only the United States, but also all of North and South America.

Expansionism led to a number of dilemmas and questions, both practical and moral. The country grew quickly, particularly with the Louisiana Purchase. This led to a number of questions, particularly regarding the use of land, and the designation of land for use by particular groups. There were significant arguments over whether new lands should be slave-holding or non-slave territories. These debates would come into play even more significantly during the years directly before the Civil War.

As white settlers moved into lands inhabited by Native Americans, the designation of land for white or Native American use became both more controversial and more difficult. Conflicts between Native tribes and settlers were more common as white settlers pushed into the west. The federal government increased its control of Native populations and there were a number of battles between the United States and Native American groups.

The FIRST SEMINOLE WAR, from 1816–1819, pitched America against both the Spanish and the Seminole people in parts of modern-day Florida. Spain ceded Florida to the United States in 1821, but there would be two more Seminole Wars in this time period.

The INDIAN REMOVAL ACT OF 1830, signed by Andrew Jackson, allowed for the forcible removal of the "Five Civilized Tribes" from the southern states to lands further west. These tribes included the Chickasaw, Choctaw, Muskogee-Creek, Seminole, and Cherokee. You are likely more familiar with the impact of the Indian Removal Act— the TRAIL OF TEARS or the forced resettlement of these tribes. A significant number of those resettled died on the Trail of Tears, with estimates ranging from 2,000 to 6,000 Cherokee killed (out of approximately 16,500 individuals.)

The Seminole refused to cooperate with the Indian Removal Act, leading to the Second Seminole War. The Seminole fought hard to retain their freedom, even gaining sympathy from many who questioned the actions of Jackson's government. Eventually, the Seminole remaining in Florida were pushed onto a reservation or moved west, and their population was totally eliminated from the state.

The War of 1812 and Tecumseh's War

THE WAR OF 1812 is recognized by the United States as a war in its own right, but in Britain it is remembered as part of the Napoleonic Wars that raged across Europe and Asia from 1803 to 1815. There were a number of significant battles during the War of 1812, both naval battles and on American soil. On land, the war was fought in the Deep South and along the U.S. and Canadian borders, particularly in the Great Lakes region, with several failed American attempts to invade Canada. By the end of the war, Canada remained in British control, but the United States successfully managed to defend its borders. The United States also successfully eliminated British influence among Native American tribes in the United States.

DID YOU KNOW?
The original White House and the Capitol building were burned down during the war in 1814.

Francis Scott Key penned THE STAR SPANGLED BANNER after witnessing fighting between American and British troops during the War of 1812. It was later adopted as the U.S. national anthem.

The United States didn't just fight British forces during the War of 1812. It also contended with the armies of the TECUMSEH CONFEDERACY, a diverse group of warriors from tribes all across the West and the South marshaled by the Native American leader Tecumseh.

Tecumseh fought the United States to establish an independent nation for Native American tribes. Tecumseh's War ended in 1813 with Tecumseh's execution.

The Battle of New Orleans was the last major fight in the War of 1812, and when future U.S. President Andrew Jackson's bravery made him a war hero. The War of 1812 officially ended with the TREATY OF GHENT.

One major consequence of the War of 1812 was the implosion of the Federalist Party. Federalists opposed the war and, from positions of power in New England state legislatures, prevented many northeastern states from providing soldiers to the war effort. After the war, the Era of Good Feelings produced a nationalistic mood in the country that caused the Federalist Party to collapse.

The Ascendancy of the Federal Government

Throughout the early nineteenth century, the power of the federal government grew significantly, gaining power over the states. While some were supportive of this growing federalism, there were many who objected. Even some in the Federalist Party objected to the changes in the national government, as well as to U.S. actions in the War of 1812. In 1814, Federalists in New England recognized that their party was quickly collapsing, and met to discuss strategy in a meeting now known as the **HARTFORD CONVENTION**, where they discussed an end to the Three-Fifths Compromise in the Constitution, questioned the Louisiana Purchase, and even whether to push for New England's secession from the United States. Though the Federalist Party soon came to an end, their debated illustrate the questions around expansionism and federal power at the time.

In 1832, the **NULLIFICATION CRISIS** occurred in response to a tariff passed in 1828. The Tariff of 1828 was protective, but designed particularly to benefit northern, industrialized states. It had a significant negative effect on the southern states and in the south was called the Tariff of Abominations. When Jackson was elected President, there was a clear expectation that he would reduce or eliminate the tariff; he compromised by proposing the Tariff of 1832, which had wide backing in both the North and South, but some states refused to abide by the new law. The state of South Carolina continued to oppose the Tariff of 1832, and North Carolina declared that both the Tariffs of 1828 and 1832 were unconstitutional by passing the Nullification Act. They refused to enforce the tariffs, leading the government to prepare to use force against the states. South Carolina eventually accepted a new compromise Tariff of 1833, bringing the crisis to an end, but it was a harbinger of a growing animosity between the North and South over the role of the federal government and the rights of states.

The Mason-Dixon Line

Abolitionism grew during this period, but so too did slavery. For the purposes of the AP U.S. History exam, you should fully understand the political actions concerning slavery during this period.

In 1820, the Missouri Compromise created the **MASON-DIXON LINE**, delineating a border between slave and free states. The Mason-Dixon Line ran along the 36°30' line; as this was the southern border of Missouri. Missouri was admitted as a slave state and Maine was admitted as a free state. The Missouri Compromise held until 1854.

Throughout the first half of the nineteenth century, slavery spread west through the southern half of the country, including the southern territories acquired in the Louisiana

Purchase. Agriculture drained the soils of the southeast, so slave holders moved further west in search of more fertile land, along with their slaves.

CHAPTER FIVE
A House Divided
1844–1877

There were a variety of factors that impacted the growth of American sectionalism, including slavery, states' rights, and nullification. The United States experienced significant political change that led to shifts in the organizational structures of political parties (resulting in the creation of the Republican Party) and the election of Abraham Lincoln.

North and South

To understand the events leading to war, you must understand the strong differences between the northern and southern states. They differed in culture, education, ethnicity, wealth, and more. Life was different, for both the upper and lower classes between North and South. These differences strongly impacted attitudes toward slavery, particularly as the South's support for slavery grew.

The North was, by the middle of the nineteenth century, heavily industrialized. Steel production, coal mining, and textile factories were prominent industries in the Northeast, while further west, agriculture remained commonplace. Even in agricultural communities, the local town was important. Education was relatively available, even in more rural areas. Most people were not isolated, whether they worked in a more urban setting or lived a rural life. Small farmers worked their own land, occasionally with the help of hired hands.

The population of the North was growing, both through natural reproduction and immigration. Large numbers of immigrants were arriving, taking on the industrial jobs common in the Northeast. From the 1840s onward, many of these immigrants were Irish. Discrimination against Irish immigrants was common; many businesses hung signs stating "No Irish need apply." Immigrants often lived in tenement communities in the cities, taking on difficult work with few labor protections. They were supported by religious organizations, particularly the Catholic Church. Over time, the Catholic Church's hierarchy filled with Irish priests and bishops, who created parochial schools and offered support and community for the new immigrants.

Abolitionism was growing; however, it continued to be dominated by relatively few individuals. These people, including former slaves like Frederick Douglass, spoke out and shared their experiences in writing. Church pulpits provided an outlet for abolitionists, as did print materials. Their message spread and gained political power during the years directly before the war. Following the end of slavery in the West Indies around 1830, abolitionists became progressively more outspoken. Some, like HARRIET TUBMAN, began to work actively, for example, helping escaped slaves along the Underground Railroad. In 1852, Harriet Beecher Stowe published the novel, *Uncle Tom's Cabin*. For many readers, this novel truly illustrated the evils of slavery for the first time. Stowe had witnessed slavery herself only briefly, but felt driven by her religious sentiments to speak out. Others began to believe, and share, the reality that it might take war to free the slaves in the South. Eventually, with the ascendancy of the Republican Party, the abolitionists gained essential political power.

While the North's populace broadly supported an end to slavery, African-Americans still, in many cases, lacked basic rights in the North and experienced significant discrimination, including racist minstrel shows performed throughout the North in blackface or by white actors wearing makeup to appear African-American.

Though the North had a swelling population, large cities, significant numbers of immigrants, growing industry, and improving access to education, the South did not experience any of these changes. Fewer than four percent of those living in the South were born outside of America. Most Southerners did not own slaves. In fact, only 1,400 families owned more than 100 slaves and only about one quarter of Southern families owned slaves at all. Nonetheless, support for slavery extended through all social classes,

DID YOU KNOW?
There is a single exception to the widespread support of slavery in the South—whites living in the Appalachian Mountains supported the Union during the war, did not own slaves, and did not support slave ownership.

regardless of personal involvement with slave ownership. Slavery allowed poor whites to work their own land, commonly farming corn and hogs and living in a very isolated way, with few interactions with others. The division between rich and poor was quite clear in the South. While the North was experiencing growth in the middle classes, this was not paralleled in the South. Access to jobs and education was limited for all but the wealthy classes in the South. Even for the poorest among them, the doctrine of racial superiority was key to their personal identity.

Southern culture was dominated by the large plantation owners, particularly cotton plantations. These individuals, sometimes called the cottonocracy, lived a life akin to that of the European aristocracy. They had little to do with poor Southern whites, were served by slaves, and lived a life of luxury. Their sons were typically educated in the North or abroad. Plantation families lived richly and comfortably. They were served by house slaves, with the woman of the house managing the house slaves. The field slaves were supervised by a hired white overseer, rather than a member of the family in most cases.

Black enslaved people were often viewed as valuable property, particularly for strong and healthy men or women who had a large number of children. They suffered under a racist system. Even in the best of circumstances, enslaved people lacked the right to legally marry, lacked rights to their children, could not learn to read, and could only become free with the permission of their "owner." In many cases, even minor violations of the rules were punished with whipping. Women were raped by owners or overseers. Children and families were often divided.

In the Deep South, slaves retained more of their traditional African culture. Children were typically raised by their mothers in stable, two-parent households. Christianity was prominent, and it incorporated aspects of African culture that are still present in some largely African American denominations. There were free African Americans in the South; however, they were often at risk of being captured and sold as slaves. Some free African Americans, often those of mixed race, owned property, particularly in New Orleans.

The South developed a strong ideology supporting slavery. This pro-slavery philosophy resulted in a progressive strengthening of abolitionism in the North. According to Southern propaganda, slavery was, in fact, good for the slaves: They got plenty of fresh air and sunshine, were cared for in their old age, were Christians, and did not have to worry about starvation or unemployment. Moreover, Southern propaganda touted the unscientific, but widely believed, doctrines of racial superiority suggesting that slaves were incapable of learning or education. They were contrasted with the immigrants in the North who rarely saw sunlight, lived in tenements and often died in poverty, with little access to food or shelter. While enslaved people and African Americans were viewed in general by powerful whites as lesser, wealthier Southerners had experienced close personal interactions with African Americans. Wealthy white children were frequently raised by slaves and alongside them. They often thought of those close associates with personal fondness, while still retaining strongly negative racial views.

During the years directly before the war, efforts were made to create compromises between North and South designed to maintain the union and avoid war. These compromises managed the issue of slave and free states, and the rights of slave holders, as well as states' rights.

The COMPROMISE OF 1850 was created to manage issues surrounding the admission of California to the United States, designating the borders of Texas, as well as estab-lishing the future entry of Utah and New Mexico into the United States. Negotiated by Senators John Calhoun and Henry Clay, the Compromise admitted California to the United States as a free state, placed no restrictions on slavery in Utah and New Mexico, allowing the issue to be decided by popular sovereignty, and removed New Mexico from Texas. It also banned the slave trade (but not slavery) in Washington D.C., and strengthened the Fugitive Slave Act. The **FUGITIVE SLAVE ACT** reduced the potential for escaped slaves to reach freedom, as it required that Northerners return runaway slaves.

In 1854, the **KANSAS-NEBRASKA ACT** brought an end to the Missouri Compromise of 1820 by allowing two states, both north of the Mason-Dixon Line, to choose whether or not slavery was acceptable by vote of the population. Supported by Southerners, the Act led to significant violence in the state of Kansas. In 1856, Southerners rioted and burned the town of Lawrence, Kansas.

The Kansas-Nebraska Act contributed to the growth of abolitionism and the Republican Party. **ABRAHAM LINCOLN** gave an impassioned speech in 1854 about the Kansas-Nebraska Act, in which he denounced indifference to slavery among his fellow Americans.

Southerners expected that Kansas would be settled by Southerners and become a slave state, but anti-slavery forces were successful, as a relatively large number of Northerners moved into the state, and Kansas was admitted as a free state in 1861.

The **DRED SCOTT DECISION**, or *Scott v. Sanford*, was decided by the U.S. Supreme Court in 1857. Dred Scott was a slave that had been taken to a free state by his owner. He sued for his freedom. After some ten years of deliberations, the Supreme Court decided that African-Americans could not be citizens of the United States, whether born into slavery or not, and that they did not have the right to sue in federal court or vote in elections.

Notably, the Chief Justice, Taney, was from the slave state of Maryland. The constitutional amendments following the Civil War specifically addressed the findings of this court case to nullify the Dred Scott decision.

Each of these three key decisions met the needs of the South, but served to incite strong feelings in the North. As the south gained rights, the movement for abolition grew and spread in the north.

Following the 1854 Kansas-Nebraska Act, Northerners began to organize, specifically in response to the influx of slave-owning Southerners to Kansas and Nebraska. Anti-slavery politicians met in Michigan in 1854 and the Republican Party was organized and active by 1856. The Republican Party had its roots in the Free Soil Party, whose political platform stated that a free state was morally and economically superior to one that relied upon slavery. The Republican Party was not the only threat to the traditional two-party system during this time. The 1850s also saw a strong anti-immigrant sentiment, particularly anti-Irish. This led to the creation of the short-lived Know-Nothing Party, which advocated limited naturalization and immigration and favored the rights of those born in America.

In 1858, Abraham Lincoln gave a famous speech, now known as "A House Divided," which portended the looming Civil War. He won election to the Senate from his home state of Illinois after a series of broad, free-ranging debates with his opponent, Stephen Douglas.

When Lincoln ran for president, many Southerners believed that if he won, it would lead to secession. Notably, while Lincoln was in favor of Free Soil policies, he was, as of 1865, willing to consider financial compensation for owners when slaves were freed. In the election of 1860, approximately sixty percent of the popular vote went to other candidates, but of the four running for President, Lincoln received the greatest share and became the sixteenth President of the United States.

Secession and Civil War

Four days after Lincoln's election, South Carolina called a convention to discuss the issue of secession. In December 1860, the state of South Carolina seceded from the United States. Six more states, including Mississippi, Alabama, Georgia, Texas, Louisiana, and Florida followed in the next few weeks. Eventually, four more states would secede, forming the CONFEDERATE STATES OF AMERICA in February 1861. JEFFERSON DAVIS, a former senator from the state of Mississippi, was chosen as the first president of the Confederacy, and the city of Montgomery, Alabama, was chosen as its capital.

Southerners were broadly supportive of secession, overwhelmingly because of the issue of slavery. Yet, there were other factors that informed the states' decisions to formally secede:

▶ The South had no expectation of armed action from the North. At the time of secession, the North had a relatively small standing army, and most of the soldiers were occupied in the West.

▶ Southerners were tired of abolitionist propaganda and feared the potential of slave rebellion.

▶ The North relied upon raw materials produced in the South, particularly cotton. Southerners believed that the North would be unwilling to bear the financial burden of this loss.

▶ Some in the South saw the potential to develop a new industrial economy as an independent country.

▶ The South expected foreign aid from Britain, but did not receive help. Britain had a large surplus of imported cotton and would, once the Emancipation Proclamation was issued, refuse to help slave owners. Some Southern battleships were built in Britain.

When Lincoln took office, he was faced with a country divided by secession. Some in the U.S. Senate, including Kentucky Senator Henry Crittenden, attempted a compromise along the lines of the Missouri Compromise; however, Lincoln refused to consider any compromise that supported the continuation of slavery in the United States.

War did not begin at once. In fact, Lincoln stated that the Union would not engage in military action unless forced. Secession created a number of problems, for both North and South. Logistically, the nation no longer stood as a world power, and the North was saddled with the entirety of the national debt. In the South, lacking the Fugitive Slave Act, slaves would only have to cross the Ohio River, rather than escape to Canada, to reach freedom. When the Southern states seceded, they claimed rights to federal property located in their states, including forts and arsenals. This included the valuable harbor of Fort Sumter, South Carolina.

Jefferson Davis sent his Vice President, Alexander Stephens, to woo Virginia. On April 17th, Virginia seceded from the Union and on April 2nd, the capital of the Confederacy moved from Montgomery, AL to Richmond, VA.

In April, 1861, Lincoln sent a naval force to provision the Union soldiers stationed in Fort Sumter. Confederate forces assaulted Fort Sumter and forced its surrender, thus giving Lincoln a justification to go to war. He sent a call out to Union states for troops. The South also called for troops, and the final four states—Arkansas, Tennessee, Virginia, and North Carolina—joined the Confederacy.

Slavery continued in four border states that remained part of the Union; Missouri, Kentucky, Delaware, and Maryland. The federal government worked actively and quickly to retain these states in the Union, eventually exempting them even from the Emancipation Proclamation. Lincoln reportedly said "I hope to have God on my side, but I must have Kentucky."

The stated aim of the Civil War was not, at this time, to free the slaves. Lincoln stated that it was about preserving the Union and about the Constitution. While this was a war that split North and South, some Northerners fought with the Confederacy, as did members of some Native American tribes. Some Southerners crossed state lines to fight for the Union. It was a complicated, fraught period of American history that divided not only the nation, but states, cities, church congregations, and even families.

Early in the war, the South appeared to have several clear advantages. Southerners were more accustomed to handling horses and rifles, were fighting on their home soil, and had the advantage of excellent military leadership from figures such as Generals **ROBERT E. LEE** and **STONEWALL JACKSON**. While the South lacked large-scale industry, it did seize federal armories, and built ironworks to meet their weaponry needs.

What the South could tout in morale, martial talent, and leadership, the North could tout in manpower, economy, control of the seas, and significantly more farmland devoted to growing food. Immigrants and freed slaves also joined Union troops, providing additional manpower. While there were more potential soldiers available in the North, they were less prepared for war. The North also lacked the strong military leaders of the South, and Lincoln cycled through several ineffective commanders until settling on **ULYSSES S. GRANT,** who would go on to win the Presidency after the war.

Since the Civil War was fought in the South, Northerners were at a far lower risk of shortages. In fact, the North experienced significant surpluses of wheat and corn during these years, and even exported grain to Britain. Lincoln not only had the advantage of a strong economy, but of a united government. He was able to act quickly, often without Congress, to achieve his aims during the war.

With all of its advantages, the Union expected a quick victory, and adopted an offensive-minded strategy of constant, consistent attacks on Confederate territory. The South proved, however, to be a wilier foe than the Union imagined.

DID YOU KNOW?
The Battle of Antietam on September 17, 1862, was the bloodiest single-day battle in American history, with more than 22,000 casualties.

During the course of 1861 and 1862, the South secured a number of victories; however, their limited manpower was already becoming problematic. Conscription was introduced in the Confederacy in April, 1862.

On January 1, 1863, Lincoln issued the **EMANCIPATION PROCLAMATION**, officially freeing all slaves in states rebelling against the Union. He went on to deliver the **GETTYSBURG ADDRESS** in November of the same year.

The **BATTLE OF GETTYSBURG** marked a shift in the tide of the war toward the Union's favor. By the middle of 1864, the Confederacy was weakening. The city of Atlanta fell to General Sherman in September and Savannah fell in December of 1864.

On April 9, 1865, Robert E. Lee surrendered at the Appomattox Courthouse in Virginia, acceding to Lincoln's demands that:

▶ the South abolish slavery

▶ the South adhere to the Emancipation Proclamation

▶ the Confederate troops lay down their arms

▶ the South accept the Reconstruction Amendments

Less than a week later, President Lincoln was assassinated by John Wilkes Booth, an actor and Southern sympathizer, at Ford's Theater in Washington, D.C.

Below, you'll find a brief timeline of some of the key battles in the Civil War, as well as their outcome, and any essential additional information.

▶ July 21, 1861. The battle of Bull Run resulted in a decisive Southern victory, led by Stonewall Jackson. The victory caused some Southerners to believe the war was won, leading to overconfidence and a lack of volunteers for the Confederate Army, which was already at disadvantage due to a lack of manpower.

▶ June to July, 1862. The Seven Days' Battle again resulted in Southern victory, this time led by Robert E. Lee. This victory led to increased Northern aggression and the determination to end slavery and destroy the institutions of the South – at this time, the North began consistently and constantly attacking Confederate-held territory.

- After the Seven Days' Battle, new, more aggressive Northern strategies also included the naval blockade of goods to the confederacy, securing control of the Mississippi River, and forcing Southern forces to engage in battle on multiple fronts, stretching their numbers thin.

- September 17, 1862. The Battle of Antietam Creek, Maryland caused Lee to retreat, but Lincoln removed McClellan for incompetence for failing to pursue the South's commanding general. Shortly after Antietam, Lincoln issued the Emancipation Proclamation, and many slaves joined Union forces.

- July 1-July 3, 1863. The Battle of Gettysburg resulted in a decisive Union victory, turning the direction of the war.

- November 1863. General Grant took control of Tennessee, opening the path to Georgia.

- September to December 1864. Sherman took Atlanta and Savannah.

Reconstruction

The efforts toward **RECONSTRUCTION** and reuniting the country began before the official end of the Civil War. While the North emerged from the war relatively economically strong, the South was by and large destroyed. Cities had been sacked and burned, there were few agricultural resources remaining, and there was little infrastructure.

As part of the terms of surrender, Southerners were forced to accept what are now known as the Reconstruction Amendments These were:

- The Thirteenth Amendment abolished the practice of slavery in the United States. The Thirteenth Amendment also negated the Three-Fifths Compromise.

- The Fourteenth Amendment established the due process and equal protection clauses, as well as the privileges and immunities clauses.

- The Fifteenth Amendment prohibited states from passing certain voting restrictions on citizens based on race

Despite their defeat, Southerners largely still supported secession, and the military elite and Confederate government were considered traitors. Slaves were now free African-Americans, but their social and political status remained unclear in many ways, despite the Reconstruction Amendments. The process of freedom was a very slow one, with some slaves remaining loyal to their masters, and others embracing their freedom more quickly, joining Union troops in pillaging the homes of their masters.

While freed slaves were no longer property, they lacked many services to support a transition into a free life. There were some African-American communities in towns, helping to provide jobs and access to housing and other needs. Many emancipated slaves began to look for lost relatives or move westward. These **EXODUSTERS**, or former slaves participating in the Exodus of 1879, sought a new and better life. Others stayed in the South, opening their own churches and schools to create communities, provide education, and form a network of support. Congress created the **FREEDMEN'S BUREAU** to provide a path to education and help to meet basic needs.

Lincoln intended a gentle Reconstruction policy toward the south, but his assassination enraged Northerners, and would not be satisfied with the South's unconditional surrender. Andrew Johnson, a man widely regarded as incompetent and ill-prepared for the office, proposed an ineffective Reconstruction plan, and Southern states were readmitted to the Union with few requirements to prevent them from cooperating with the goals and aims of the Union.

Without interference from Johnson, many Southern governments established the **BLACK CODES** almost at once. The Black Codes did the following:

▶ limited the rights of African-Americans to rent or own property.

▶ allowed any white police officer to arrest a "vagrant" African-American and sentence them to involuntary servitude—essentially, re-enslaving them.

▶ disallowed African-Americans from serving on juries or otherwise engaging with the legal system.

▶ set penalties for African-Americans who left labor contracts, the terms of which were often semantically equal to slavery.

▶ barred African-Americans from voting.

The Black Codes were not the sole issue impacting the Southern states and the response from the North. Upon re-entering the Union, a number of states sent representatives to Congress. Many of those they chose were former Confederate generals or otherwise involved in the secession. The new census counts, including free African-Americans, increased the proportion of Southern Democrats in the Republican-controlled House, causing significant legislative issues for the newly reunited country.

Constitutional Changes

The **THIRTEENTH AMENDMENT** abolished slavery throughout the United States. Passed after the Emancipation Proclamation, but before the end of the Civil War, the Thirteenth Amendment was first passed in April 1864 by the Senate and became law after the end of the war, in December 1865. The amendment was ratified by the required two-third majority, including the Union states, border states, and some re-admitted Southern states. The Thirteenth Amendment is relatively straightforward and has had little impact on later judicial decisions. It did, however, provide critical protections for former slaves.

The **Fourteenth Amendment**, ratified in 1868, guarantees citizenship to all individuals born in the United States or naturalized as citizens in the United States. States lack any right to limit the rights of citizens, according to the Fourteenth Amendment. This amendment also limits the rights of anyone who has participated in rebellion, disallowing them from serving in a political capacity without the specific permission of two-thirds of the House and Senate. The Fourteenth Amendment also eliminates any federal responsibility for debts incurred during rebellion or insurrection and allows the federal government to enforce voting rights. While the Thirteenth Amendment has a limited impact on later legislation and judiciary decisions, the Fourteenth has been key to a number of judicial decisions. The Due Process clause has been used to apply the Bill of Rights to states' laws, while the Equal Protection clause formed the basis of desegregation in the United States nearly a century later.

The **Fifteenth Amendment** guaranteed voting rights to all male citizens, regardless of race or freedom at birth. Ratified in 1870, this is the last of the Reconstruction Amendments. While the Fifteenth Amendment provided for voting rights, later judicial decisions did not support the Fifteenth Amendment, allowing a number of restrictions on voting rights. These restrictions include literacy tests, poll taxes, and grandfather clauses.

Congress also created the Freedmen's Bureau during this period, hoping to stem the Black Codes in the Southern states. While the women's rights movements and abolitionism were closely linked, women were not granted either full citizenship or the right to vote with the Reconstruction Amendments.

Expanionsit Foreign Policy

During the first half of the nineteenth century, the United States embarked on a policy of **EXPANSIONISM**. This was marked by several goals, both political and economic. The country wanted to secure control over lands previously under the control of European powers, support young democracies in Latin America, and gain new economic rights and trading privileges. By the middle of the century, the United States was both a world power and a growing destination for migrants, with large numbers leaving Europe for the United States.

Manifest destiny continued to guide U.S. policy. This belief in American superiority was key to policy decisions, but it was not only a belief in cultural superiority. There was also, for many Americans, a racist component. Many believed that manifest destiny also held that white Americans—rather than new immigrants—were at the helm of America's destiny, and that their needs could outweigh those of others, particularly Native Americans, African-Americans, and many immigrant groups.

Prior to the Civil War, large numbers of immigrants entered the country. Most of these immigrants were European; however, this did not eliminate discrimination. In the broadest of terms, those that were white Protestants were largely accepted, with little discrimination. Immigrants from Catholic countries were much less accepted. There were strong anti-Catholic movements in the United States. These can be seen in the treatment of both Irish and, later, Italian immigrants. During this period, bias against the Irish was particularly strong; however, German Catholic immigrants were also discriminated against. Politically, many feared the potential influence of the Catholic Pope on the political views of new immigrants. The **KNOW-NOTHING MOVEMENT** of the 1850s, originally called the Native American Party, was a political movement designed to limit the rights of ethnic and religious minorities, as well as their potential political influence. They wanted to limit immigration and make citizenship more difficult. Membership in the Know Nothing movement was limited to white, Protestant men.

While there was significant discrimination against Catholic immigrants, they made a place for themselves within the American landscape. Catholic parishes helped to preserve local languages, provided Catholic education through parochial schools, and served as an essential community support for new immigrants. The parochial schools did not receive government funding, but were considered essential by Catholic immigrant communities, helping to create a Catholic identity and prevent the conversion of immigrant children to Protestantism. For instance, a new Polish immigrant would find a Polish-speaking Catholic church in his community, send his children to a Polish and English-speaking parochial school, and often, make his way in his community with the aid of his parish church. The parish system, so closely connected to the Catholic Church, can also be seen in less immigrant-friendly areas, like New Orleans, because of its long Catholic history as a French and Spanish settlement. Over the course of the nineteenth century, the Irish came to dominate the American Catholic Church.

With regard to expansionism in this period, students should see it as a continuation of the types of expansionism discussed in the previous chapter. American settlers pushed westward, limiting the amount of land available for Native Americans and progressively engaging in more violent conflicts with Native American tribes in the area. Southerners also pushed westward, taking slave ownership with them.

International trade grew significantly, expanding into different regions as America developed new trade relationships. Several factors contributed to the growth of substantial international trade.

- ▶ Clipper ships, first developed in the late eighteenth century, were relatively small, fast sailing ships, used for international crossings and predominantly produced in the United States and Britain. These ships could not carry large amounts of heavy cargo, but could move smaller, luxury goods relatively quickly. Clipper ships are particularly associated with the tea and opium trades.

- ▶ During this period, the United States forced the opening of trade and diplomatic relationships with traditionally isolated Japan. U.S. Commodore

Matthew Perry took a large, well-armed frigate to Japan in 1852. Under threat of force, he initiated diplomatic relations. This led to the 1854 Convention of Kanagawa, signed by the Japanese Shogun. The Convention of Kanagawa allowed for trade, foreign concessions, and specified treatment for Americans living on Japanese soil. This treaty was eventually a key factor that led to the end of the Shogunate and the Meiji Restoration in Japan.

▶ Protestant missionaries moved to Asia in larger numbers than ever before during this period. Treaties in 1842 and 1860 opened up much of China to American missionaries, allowing them to open schools, churches, and spread not only their religious values, but also their cultural values.

Westward Migration Continues

Settlers continued to move west, seeking out access to homesteads, the ability to create new communities, and even wealth in the gold mines of the west. While many of these settlers were white, others were not. Free African-Americans moved west in search of a better life, along with members of religious minorities. Some immigrant groups established communities in the western territories. For instance, even today, southern Minnesota and western Wisconsin retain close cultural ties to the early Swedish pioneers who settled these areas beginning in the middle of the nineteenth century.

The government actively supported the settlement of the west, particularly by white settlers; however, homesteading was available to other individuals as well. Laws helped to encourage families to move west. The first laws designed to award lands in the west were intended specifically to encourage family farms, rather than larger farms worked by slaves.

The Homestead Acts were a series of laws granting land to individuals who worked the land at little or no cost. They were designed to encourage family farms, rather than large, slave-worked plantations.

DID YOU KNOW?

Homesteaders frequently moved west with nothing more than they could carry in a wagon, ideally arriving at their new home with time to build an adequate cabin before winter, as well as shelter for their animals. In order to homestead, a family had to have enough wealth to see them through the first lean years, particularly the first year, before their land began to produce.

Land could be claimed in 160-acre parcels, but there were specific rules regarding who could claim land and under what conditions. The **HOMESTEAD ACT OF 1862** allowed anyone who had never taken up arms against the government, including women and freed slaves, to claim land. Individuals had to be at least twenty-one years old or the head of a household to qualify as homesteaders and often had to meet residency requirements, typically living for five years on the land and improving it. Kansas, in particular, was home to many former slaves. Kansas was relatively close to the south, limiting the length of the journey, and had a long history of supporting abolition, making it an appealing destination and home for newly freed African-Americans. There were a number of later changes to the laws, expanding them to help manage issues of Reconstruction in the South and allow larger parcels of land in specific territories or circumstances.

With its origins in the early nineteenth century in New York, the growing Church of Jesus Christ of the Latter-Day Saints moved progressively westward. Officially founded in 1830 in Ohio, Mormons were forced to move west to escape persecution. Not long after the 1830 founding, a second branch began in Missouri, so Mormon settlers moved west to Missouri after being forced from Ohio. Conflict with local people continued, eventually leading to the death of the founder, Joseph Smith. Some 60,000 Mormons then made a 1,000 mile journey west, led by Brigham Young. Following the promulgation of the doctrine of plural marriage or polygamy, conflicts between the U.S. government and Mormon settlers increased, particularly as Utah sought statehood. The Mormons settled many areas in the west, but are most closely associated with Utah, still the primary center for the Church of Jesus Christ of the Latter-Day Saints today.

Land and religious freedom were not the only pull factors drawing settlers to the west. One of the most significant factors in mass migration west was the **GOLD RUSH**. In 1848, James W. Marshall found gold in Coloma, California. News spread, first into Oregon, but eventually, all the way east. The first to seek gold, and the wealthiest, were the "forty-eighters". These were largely local Californians, both white and Spanish-speaking, as well as people from relatively nearby, like Mexico. By 1849, Americans were moving west, but so were many others, including Asians coming from the east. While the gold rush is often associated with male migration, many women moved to California, either to accompany their husbands and families, or even to seek their own fortunes. Early in the gold rush, gold could be picked up off the ground, creating wealthy men almost overnight. Gold panning, using simple sifters in mountain streams, followed. Later in the gold rush, more sophisticated and intensive mining techniques were used. In fewer than six years, the city of San Francisco appeared from nothing more than a very small town. In total, more than 300,000 people joined the gold rush of the 1840s and 1850s.

DID YOU KNOW?
While Oregon was under U.S. control, much of California, particularly southern California, was under Mexican control.

As noted, not all gold seekers were white settlers. Once the initial rush ended around 1850, American gold seekers began to object to foreigners, particularly Latin Americans and Asians. Discriminatory taxes against foreign gold miners were implemented in Northern California; however, there were also acts of violence against non-American and non-white gold miners.

The huge influx of new residents with the gold rush significantly impacted another population; local Native Americans. The gold rush of California took place in a region inhabited by Native Americans who subsisted largely through hunting and fishing. Violence between miners and Native American groups resulted in massacres of Native American villages by gold miners.

As white settlers moved west, they displaced populations in those regions, including Native Americans and Hispanics. Violence, both small- and large-scale, was quite common. These conflicts were widespread throughout the west.

In California, Mexican governor Mariano Guadalupe Vallejo welcomed a group of Americans, signing an agreement allowing them access to California in exchange for not taking him or his family prisoner. This agreement was ignored, and Vallejo and a number of others were imprisoned at Sutter's Fort. Initially, they were treated relatively well; however, later they were treated as any other prisoner. Vallejo was eventually released, after offering his support to the Americans. By the time of his capture, the United States already controlled Northern California, and soon controlled Southern California, as well.

Conflicts in the West

The **Sand Creek Massacre** of November 29, 1864 is one of many atrocities committed by the United States against Native Americans during the settlement of the West. Conditions in the Colorado territory were tumultuous. The Dakota people revolted in 1862 and 1863, increasing tensions between Native Americans and white settlers; however, the scope and horror of the violence in November 1864 marks one of the worst moments of this period. An army of 675 volunteer soldiers, led by Colonel John M. Chivington, attacked a Cheyenne and Arapahoe village in Southeastern Colorado. The village had a population of around 700 people in total, many of them women, children, and elderly. Chivington's army attacked the village, but many managed to escape by digging trenches near a stream. The troops continued to attack the fleeing villagers, many of whom were non-combatants. By the end of the day, they had killed approximately 200 villagers. Before moving on the following day, the soldiers defiled the bodies of the dead.

The **Battle of Little Big Horn** in June, 1876 is one of the best known conflicts between U.S. forces and Native Americans (Lakota Sioux and Cheyenne in this case). It is also one of the last significant armed attempts by Native American tribes to preserve their traditional way of life and use of land. The Sioux and Cheyenne were both horse cultures, following migratory herds of buffalo and relying upon the buffalo for sustenance. In 1868, some Lakota agreed to move onto reservations; however, others, including well-known leaders like Sitting Bull, refused. In June 1876, Sitting Bull predicted a great victory. The battalions of the Seventh Calvary were sent out to eliminate groups and bands of Lakota Sioux and Cheyenne. All of these tribes were nomadic, moving regularly. The Seventh Calvary was prepared for a group of up to 1,500 warriors, as well as any women and children that might be part of the tribe. In total, the village at Little Big Horn River contained around 8,000 people, including 1,500 to 1,800 warriors. The Lakota Sioux were victorious at Little Big Horn and more than 250 U.S. soldiers died in the fighting, including Lt. Colonel Armstrong Custer. This was the last significant victory for the Lakota Sioux in the battles for the Great Plains.

CHAPTER SIX
The Second Industrial Revolution
1865–1898

The latter part of the nineteenth century is typically identified as the SECOND INDUS- TRIAL REVOLUTION. If the first was driven by coal and steam, the second was driven by steel. New immigrants, often from Southern and Eastern Europe, worked in the steel factories of the East Coast. Toward the interior of the nation, new resources were mined, including coal, oil, and iron. Cities grew throughout the country and more and more people entered the wage-earning workforce, leaving rural family farms for city life. While women worked in textile factories early in the Industrial Revolution, they now found a place in offices, working at switchboards, in department stores, or as secretaries. In most cases, women only worked until marriage.

While some individuals moved up and into the middle class, many others, particularly new immigrants, lived in urban slums. Conditions in the slums were horrific, with a high spread of disease, pest infestation, and overcrowding. These slums lacked adequate air, hygiene, sanitation, or space. Often large numbers of people lived in only a single room, with shared toilet facilities or none at all. Flophouses were left to the poorest of all, where for a few cents, someone could sleep for a few hours.

Resources were not the only factor driving this revolution. Mass production, first devised by ELI WHITNEY, also changed the way goods were produced, improving the efficiency of American factories. New technology appeared, making production and conducting business easier than ever before. Innovations dating to this period, created by inventors like THOMAS EDISON, include:

- ▶ Cash register, typewriter, stock ticker
- ▶ Electric railways used in cities, refrigerated cars on trains, the electric dynamo
- ▶ Telegraph, telephone
- ▶ Phonograph, moving pictures
- ▶ The electric light bulb

The Second Industrial Revolution was responsible for the creation of a new class of business tycoons. These were magnates, running large-scale industries and often buying out similar industries. In the end, a few men controlled entire areas of production, like the oil and steel industries. These millionaires created a new aristocracy, looking down on the poor and largely condemning social reforms. Even today some of these names may be familiar:

▶ Andrew Carnegie controlled the steel industry

▶ John D. Rockefeller controlled the oil industry

▶ J.P. Morgan controlled the banking industry

Many of these men, wealthy beyond measure, acquired multiple corporations in their field, gaining control of enough of the means of production to set prices. These practices eventually led to **ANTI-TRUST LEGISLATION**, passed by Teddy Roosevelt to prevent price controls, which are still used today.

After the Civil War, industry finally reached the South, with the growth of pre-rolled cigarettes and cotton production. Cotton factories were built in the South for the first time. Labor laws and organization came later to the South, and mill towns employed entire families, including children.

The Labor Movement

Conditions in factories throughout the United States were typically poor. With a large labor pool, workers were not paid fairly. Hours were long; twelve- to fourteen-hour shifts were typical in most fields. Factory machinery was dangerous, and there was frequently no support or assistance in place for individuals injured on the job.

Workers were often at the mercy of their employers. While smaller factories were typically owned by an individual or a family, now factories were controlled by large corporations, running many sites, rather than a single one. Employees had no value, and much of the labor done was unskilled without any significant training or knowledge required.

Workers began to organize, forming **LABOR UNIONS** to gain power and the ability to stand up for themselves against their employers. Labor unions grew until 1870, when a nationwide depression reduced the overall power of the unions for a period of time.

Labor unions allowed workers to strike, but still lacked power. When unions initiated strikes, corporations hired strikebreakers and engaged in violent activity with labor organizers. Many corporations required thet workers sign contracts banning labor unions and participation in organized labor. Corporations further controlled workers by creating company towns. In many cases, the company towns controlled both food and housing for the workers, creating a cycle of debt. This made it far more difficult for workers to organize or take action against an employer. Nonetheless, unions, like the

Knights of Labor, worked for better conditions, both in individual factories and on a larger scale, through legal change.

By the turn of the century, some half a million workers were part of the largest labor union, the AMERICAN FEDERATION OF LABOR or AFL.

Conservation and Agriculture

The United States was now made up of a huge amount of land, progressively more connected through railroads. A stronger federal government controlled a significant amount of this land, regulated and managed by the Department of the Interior. This included the first national parks, federally-owned land, and Native American Reservations. The federal government retained control of some valuable resources, including mining, lands for ranching, and large parcels of land that made up the available land offered by the Homestead Act. Organizations were also created to control U.S. fisheries, like the U.S. Fish Commission and to preserve wilderness areas.

The SIERRA CLUB, still well-known today, was founded during this period. This movement toward conservation often conflicted with business interests, including coal and oil production. In a minimally settled America, there was little need for conservation. As America became more urbanized, the need to preserve wilderness areas became serious.

DID YOU KNOW?
The first national park, Yellowstone National Park, was created by President Ulysses S. Grant in 1872. In 1906, Teddy Roosevelt signed the Antiquities Act and designated Devil's Point in Wyoming as the first national monument. The National Park Service would not exist until 1916, under Woodrow Wilson.

As people were moving out of rural areas and into cities, other settlers were moving into rural areas, settling the West. Changes in agricultural technology throughout the nineteenth century led fewer workers to be able to produce more food, while refrigerated train cars made transporting foods easier and safer than ever before. This mechanization of agriculture impacted both how food was produced and the people who produced it. While factory-style farms of today were not yet in use, the changes to farming made it more of an industry.

Organized labor movements impacted this industry, just as they had factory work. Farmers organized to advocate for their rights and provide support with groups like THE GRANGE. The Grange provided a means for rural farmers to organize together. Eventually, the Grange succeeded in establishing free rural mail delivery, so rural families did not have to collect their mail in town, as well as the Granger Laws, which set price limits on rail transport of grain and other agricultural products.

In Texas, the Southern Farmers' Alliance advocated for farmers' rights; however, African-American farmers were not allowed to join. In 1886, the Colored Alliance of Farmers was founded, eventually spreading throughout the South. The Colored Alliance of Farmers promoted vocational training, home ownership, and offered some support services, including discounted farming supplies, to its members.

While the Grange advocated for farmers, particularly in the Midwest, in the Southwest, Las Gorras Blancas organized to prevent land grabs and protect traditional land rights for Mexicans in the New Mexico area. They protested delays in responding to complaints, and government regulations mandating that paperwork be filed in English. In many cases, land grabs occurring under the white administration were illegal, even under the Homestead Act of 1862, and Gorras Blancas worked hard to protect the interests of its members.

Established in 1891, the People's or **POPULIST PARTY** originated in poor, agricultural regions of the southern United States. Friendly to organized labor, the Populist Party objected to big business, the railroad, and industrial power. They advocated government control of the railroads, telephone lines and other commodities, an eight-hour working day, fair labor laws, and the abolition of national banks. While women were active members in the Populist Party, leaders expressed white supremacist views. By 1896, the Democratic Party absorbed some of the causes associated with the Populist Party, and it faded from existence.

Immigration, Racism, and Women's Rights

Immigration to the United States continued, as there were no immigration laws or regulations that set limits. Those who arrived in America were generally welcomed; they could work and become citizens. Many immigrant farmers moved into the United States, including individuals from Britain, Germany, and Northern European countries like Finland, Sweden, and Norway. They continued farming as they had in their original homes, and many of these immigrants were literate and moved with some amount of material wealth, as well as close community ties. They were, unlike immigrants from Ireland and later, Italy and Eastern Europe, relatively well-accepted in their communities.

Immigrants from Southern and Eastern Europe were typically less well-educated. Many were Catholic, Orthodox, or Jewish. Most moved with few belongings and little money. Many were single men with no plans to remain in the United States; they moved to work, earn money, and send it home in the form of remittances—this lifestyle is practiced by many undocumented immigrants from Central America today.

Others who moved to seek a better life lacked the skills or community ties to smoothly transition into life in America. There were few services in place for these immigrants. Eventually, this led to rampant corruption in the city, as "bosses" leading criminal or near-criminal organizations filled needs unmet by the city, state, or federal governments. Eventually, women opened settlement houses, designed to help immigrants, particularly women and children. Settlement houses played a key role in the creation of a new profession, social work.

Growing numbers of immigrants came to the West Coast from Asia, including many from China. While there were biases and discrimination against European immigrants, they were far more tolerated than Chinese immigrants. The first immigration laws and restrictions were put in place to end immigration to the United States from China.

Immigration restrictions were largely the work of Nativist politicians. **NATIVIST POLITICIANS** said they supported the rights of those born on American soil, but in practice, they were concerned with the rights of white Protestants. They sought a variety of restrictions on immigration, particularly of groups they deemed undesirable, such as the Chinese. Early immigration restrictions disallowed access to the United States for criminals, the extremely poor, and for convicts. As of 1885, companies could not import foreign labor, but had to hire workers domestically. Later restrictions eliminated immigration by individuals carrying disease, the insane, polygamists, and prostitutes. While these restrictions were in place, they did relatively little to slow the flow of immigrants to the United States. In 1886, the people of France gave the **STATUE OF LIBERTY** to the United States, marking the port of New York City where most immigrants entered the country. The office at **ELLIS ISLAND** opened in 1892 to process new immigrants to the United States. Many of these immigrants played a key role in helping America to achieve economic, industrial, and military success. While the lives of immigrants were hard, many achieved great success.

Migration also occurred internally, within the United States, as growing numbers of settlers moved west. This led to increased conflicts with Native Americans as homesteading settlers took Native American lands, and were given ownership over those lands by the U.S. government. Past treaties between the U.S. government and Native American nations were frequently ignored. The federal government gave land to individuals through the Homestead Act and also to states. Land-grant colleges were established when the federal government granted individual states the right to sell large amounts of land to pay for the establishment of schools. The federal government also seized land owned and used by Mexican-Americans and Native Americans in the Southwest.

Native Americans were increasingly pushed onto reservations and encouraged to acclimate themselves to a traditionally European-style life. The **DAWES ACT OF 1887** was designed to encourage Native Americans to assimilate to white culture. It allowed the U.S. government to divide up reservation land, giving individuals ownership of plots of land. In doing so, individual native people would become citizens of the United States, rather than members of a sovereign Native American nation. Excess land could then be sold to profit the U.S. government.

Resistance to the U.S. government remained among Native Americans, as smaller bands fought settlers, and tribes fought being moved from their lands to reservations, often some distance from the lands they traditionally inhabited. The **NEZ-PERCE OF**

OREGON were to be moved by the U.S. military to a smaller reservation in Idaho. Some, but not all chiefs had agreed to the move, having been promised financial incentives. Those who refused to sign, including one of the tribal elders, Chief Joseph, remained on their lands. While they were attacked by settlers and military forces, the Chief did not allow any form of violence or retribution and eventually gained the admiration of those around him, including the U.S. military. Joseph consistently sought peace, even during the Nez-Perce war that followed. The Nez-Perce were attempting to reach sanctuary with the Lakota Sioux in Canada when the remaining men were forced to surrender. The men under Chief Joseph were never allowed to return to their tribe, although they did return to Idaho, where his descendants remain.

While Chief Joseph of the Nez Perce worked actively for peaceful solutions, other Native American groups found different paths to survival in a world increasingly dominated by a white government. One of these was religious. While most Native American tribes held differing religious beliefs, many shared some religious commonalities. In 1889, WOVOKA, or Jack Wilson, a Native American religious leader, began a new ritual that many believed would restore prosperity to the Native Americans—THE GHOST DANCE. The Ghost Dance spread throughout the West, inspiring Native Americans to resist moving from their lands and adopting white lifestyles. The Ghost Dance was a contributing factor to Lakota Sioux resistance at this time, eventually leading to the actions of the American military at the WOUNDED KNEE MASSACRE. Following Wounded Knee, the Ghost Dance became significantly less common.

Women continued to work for additional rights, both politically and socially. As more women entered the workforce, their economic power grew, as did their opportunities to make different choices. Growing numbers of women were seeking vocational education and pursuing work outside the home, at least for some time prior to marriage. Women also organized during this period, creating a variety of clubs and organizations that provided support, education, and other assistance for women. These included the NATIONAL AMERICAN WOMAN SUFFRAGE ASSOCIATION which worked for the right to vote and the WOMEN'S CHRISTIAN TEMPERANCE LEAGUE, which campaigned to make alcohol illegal. These groups often had political aims; within them many women found a new level of camaraderie and support.

The Women's Christian Temperance League was part of a broader organized social effort in America called the TEMPERANCE MOVEMENT. Their crowning achievement would be the enactment of PROHIBITION early in the twentieth century.

Many women took on a public role, speaking out for their rights, as well as the rights of the poor. As they had under abolition, racism and women's rights overlapped in many cases. African-American Ida B. Wells worked against lynching in the South, campaigned for women's suffrage and women's rights, and was an active voice for civil rights. Women who had worked for abolition continued their work for suffrage and civil rights, including ELIZABETH CADY STANTON, best remembered for her work at the Seneca Falls Convention of 1848. Elizabeth Cady Stanton was concerned with far more than voting rights. She also worked for property and divorce rights for women and access to birth control.

On the other hand, a number of organizations existed specifically to promote racism and religious discrimination. The **AMERICAN PROTECTIVE ASSOCIATION (APA)** was anti-Catholic, opposing Irish Catholicism in particular, continuing the trend of discrimination against the Irish earlier in the century. Founded in the 1860s, the **KU KLUX KLAN** (KKK) violently attacked African-Americans in the South. This first incarnation of the organization was relatively short-lived; however, racism continued far beyond the South.

Judicial decisions of the Supreme Court had a far more significant impact on the life of African-Americans throughout the United States, but particularly in the southern states. Some moved north or west, where they were discriminated against, but had more opportunities. The most significant case was *Plessy vs. Ferguson*. Decided in 1896, the Supreme Court deemed that racial segregation was constitutional so long as citizens were "separate but equal."

For almost a century, segregation resulted in poorer quality education, health care, and access to various public facilities for African-Americans. While segregation was not widely instituted in the North, African-Americans still were not welcome in many facilities, frequently worked lower-paid jobs, and lacked access to the resources that whites enjoyed.

There were some noted voices speaking on behalf of the African-American community during this period, including **BOOKER T. WASHINGTON**, an African-American intellectual. Educated at Alabama's Tuskegee Institute, Washington supported education and increased access to services for African-Americans, but discouraged legal challenges to segregation, because though he believed it was unjust, he believed that it would be better to end it in a conservative fashion—by showing white Americans that segregation did not benefit them, even as it was a detriment to African-Americans. He worked for economic advancement, job training, and higher education, hoping to create a class of African-American educators, doctors, merchants, and professionals. He remained the dominant voice for African-American rights until 1909, when **W.E.B DUBOIS** founded the **NATIONAL ASSOCIATION FOR THE ADVANCEMENT OF COLORED PEOPLE**, or NAACP.

The Railroad

The need for a **TRANSCONTINENTAL RAILROAD** was clear by the middle of the nineteenth century; however, the path the rail would take did not become clear until the South seceded from the Union. When the Civil War ended in 1865, the building of the rails began in earnest. The government provided land grants and some amount of funds to establish the **UNION PACIFIC RAILROAD**.

Irish immigrants and freed slaves most commonly worked for the Union Pacific line, and Chinese immigrants for the **CENTRAL PACIFIC LINE**, while white, non-Catholic workers were present on both lines.

DID YOU KNOW?
Often railroad workers conflicted with Native Americans, leading to deaths on both ends. Towns along the rails grew rapidly from small villages to cities, while communities without rail access grew smaller.

The Central Pacific moved from west to east and the Union Pacific from east to west, and there were other, smaller lines that moved north and south.

Working conditions were poor; workers lived in tent towns, called "hell on wheels," at the end of each section of rail. These rough communities were made up of supervisors, workers, as well as workers in the businesses that moved with them as they built the railroad through the wilderness—gambling houses, dance halls, and brothels.

The presence of transcontinental rail made it easier than ever to move from place to place. Migration from the cities to new regions was more accessible than ever before. Travel was also, for the first time, a viable option. Standardized time across the country appeared, in order to help keep trains on schedule.

The rails also created a new wealthy class of railroad tycoons that wielded remarkable political power, but corruption was rampant in this industry. It was during this time that the word *millionaire* came into existence.

The Gilded Age

The late nineteenth century is often called **THE GILDED AGE**, which refers to the wealth of coal, oil, and steel magnates. The wealthy in America built fine city homes, established charitable organizations, founded cultural institutions, and much more. Many in the wealthier classes believed that they deserved their wealth, and that those of the lower classes were less deserving.

Some did, however, as stated by Andrew Carnegie in *the Gospel of Wealth*, believe the rich had a responsibility to redistribute their wealth to help "the deserving poor."

While there were movements to improve the plight of the lower classes, including the labor movement, magnates and millionaires commanded Gilded Age political and economic attention. Throughout much of the nineteenth century, the government adopted economic policies designed to protect American industry, including protective tariffs. These tariffs made it more cost-effective to buy locally produced goods and encouraged exports over imports.

DID YOU KNOW?
Within America, the government maintained a *laissez-faire* or free market economic policy. Companies could set both prices and wages as they saw fit, without government interference.

As corporations expanded and corruption increased, there were growing political objections to many of these traditional economic policies. Above, you reviewed one of those responses to the big business of the Gilded Age, the Anti-Trust Act.

The **INTERSTATE COMMERCE ACT OF 1887** also served a similar role, reducing the ability of the railroads to create **MONOPOLIES** and set prices without market interference. This was the first piece of economic legislation designed to control the business community and reduce the power of industry.

The changing politics of this age, in response to public concerns about big business in the latter part of the Gilded Age, came to be known as the **PROGRESSIVE ERA**. The Progressives, while political, relied upon philosophical and economic justifications for their theories. These included the work of **HENRY GEORGE** who believed that the concentration of unearned wealth, or wealth accumulated by owning land and resources, was the main cause of poverty. George recognized that the poor on the West Coast in California were far better off than those in the cities of the East Coast. The difference was typically in land ownership. On the West Coast, the poor owned small plots of land and therefore had more resources available.

Religious organizations also attempted to address social and political issues. The **SOCIAL GOSPEL** was a Protestant organization that sought to apply religious principles of Christian ethics to social issues, including the issues impacting the poor, labor, and issues involving children. The Social Gospel was later embraced by the Progressive movement, particularly the liberal wing, but remained most popular among the clergy. The laity were less involved; however, the clergy was able to influence the political machine of the U.S. government.

While the Progressive movement was relatively well-accepted, **SOCIALISM** also grew in popularity during this period. Often connected to the labor movement, socialists publicly criticized big business, were focused on workers' rights, and often engaged in extreme political activism. Small socialist groups around the country based their views not only on socialist philosophy, but also on utopian novels, like the works of Edward Bellamy.

The socialist party in America advocated for an eight-hour workday, an end to competition, and state ownership of resources. Socialism particularly appealed to intellectuals and academics. Socialism was not well-received, but was not considered a threat or anti-American until World War I. The socialists actively opposed the war, leading to more significant opposition to socialism, particularly after the Russian Revolution.

The final decades of the nineteenth century led to significant changes in the political and economic world of the early twentieth century. The trends that began in these years continued into the pre-war decades, including Progressive politics, socialism, and the growth of business.

CHAPTER SEVEN
A Superpower Comes of Age
1890–1945

Many of the changes that began after the Civil War continued at the turn of the century, including a move toward industrialization and urbanization, the growth of large-scale corporations, and continuing social divisions between rich and poor. As the industrialized economy grew, a new focus on the production of consumer goods provided more job opportunities for both factory workers and office workers. Conditions for workers improved somewhat, particularly during the economic boom early in the twentieth century. Women continued to join the work force, but did not enter the working world in large numbers until World War I and World War II. During both world wars, women took the place of men in factories across the country, meeting essential wartime needs.

The methods of production changed with the introduction of new technologies and ways of working, like the assembly line, invented by automobile designer Henry Ford. Immigration continued in large numbers to the United States, along with population redistribution. New cities grew in the west as urbanization moved across the nation. While the Progressives instituted some business reforms, the economy remained largely free of regulation.

This led to significant alterations in the market economy during this period, from the extreme highs of the early 1920s to the extreme lows of the Great Depression. Over the course of this period, the desire for new levels of economic regulation grew to prevent these extreme lows and maintain a stable economy. Eventually, this economic intervention led to the first significant banking regulation and social welfare programs during the years following the election of Franklin D. Roosevelt to the presidency.

Progressive Change

Movements for social change did not begin with the politicians, but with the people. Journalists exposed the conditions in factories and the inner cities. Women from settlement houses shared stories of the suffering of immigrants in the cities. Organizations were formed to improve these conditions, privately or with the assistance of churches. These included the **NATIONAL CONSUMER LEAGUE**, founded by Florence Kelley in 1899. The National Consumer League campaigned for a federal minimum wage, eight-hour workdays,and child labor laws. Kelley also helped to found the NAACP with W. E. B. Dubois. Kelley was known for her willingness to fight for causes she believed in, including the right to education for all people.

The **PROGRESSIVE MOVEMENT**, which began in the latter part of the nineteenth century, became more prominent by the early twentieth century, producing three presidents and many legislators. Significant political change occurred during this period encouraged by Progressive politicians. Progressivism was an anti-corruption movement, concerned both with corporate corruption, and corruption in the less savory parts of society. Progressives instituted measures to bring down the bosses that controlled the underbelly of major cities, including bars, gambling, and prostitution.

Progressives supported the following:

▶ women's suffrage, as they were considered less corrupt or corruptible as voters

▶ labor laws, including child labor and reasonable working conditions

▶ anti-trust laws, as applied to big business

▶ prohibition, or the banning of alcohol

▶ public education, including higher education

▶ access to health care, with broad support for new hospitals and medical facilities

▶ scientific study, both in education and medicine

▶ fair competition in industry with an end to trusts

▶ free democracy, including the use of the popular vote or referendum

▶ banking regulation, including the Federal Reserve, designed to maintain the function of banks in times of crisis

Prohibition passed with the eighteenth amendment in 1920. It was unsuccessful, leading to an increase in organized crime and the rise of criminals like Al Capone. Prohibition was repealed in 1933 with the passage of the twenty-first amendment. The twenty-first amendment is the only amendment in the Constitution that repeals another.

Women gained the vote with the passage of the nineteenth amendment in 1920.

By the beginning of the twentieth century, Progressives dominated American politics, including the presidency. **THEODORE ROOSEVELT** is the best-known of the Progressives. After transforming the Republican Party, he eventually left it to form the short-lived Progressive Party in 1912.

The New Deal

While the Progressive Movement became less popular during the 1920s, the ideology of the Progressives influenced the policies of **PRESIDENT FRANKLIN D. ROOSEVELT**, who was Theodore Roosevelt's Nephew.

FDR's **NEW DEAL** was a package of programs and policies designed to help restore the American economy during the Great Depression. The three primary goals of the New Deal were "relief, recovery, and reform."

The New Deal was politically controversial. Conservatives sought to limit the New Deal, believing that a "safety net" of governmental social programs would create a federal government that was too strong, and that would eventually threaten the liberty of individual American citizens. Liberals and social reformers did not believe that the programs would go far enough to help the suffering American populace.

Roosevelt overcame political controversy by building broad public support for the New Deal through his weekly **FIRESIDE CHATS**, which broadcast directly to the radios in Americans homes.

He also had support from the Democratic Party, including southern Democrats, like Louisiana Senator **HUEY LONG**. Long instituted new programs in his home state to improve health care and education, and was known for his strong support of programs that would redistribute wealth by taxing corporations heavily and using that money to invest in the needs of the population.

Some of the most notable programs and policies of the New Deal include:

▶ The National Recovery Administration (NRA)
▶ The Tennessee Valley Authority (TVA)
▶ The Works Public Administration (WPA)
▶ The Federal Deposit Insurance Corporation (FDIC)
▶ The Civilian Conservation Corps

The **NATIONAL RECOVERY ADMINISTRATION** or NRA was formed to balance the needs of business, agriculture, and consumers. This imbalance was viewed as a significant part of the cause of the Depression. Goals included creating fair competition, establishing minimum wages, and creating a balanced market economy less likely to encounter significant fluctuations like those that led to the Depression. In 1935 the NRA was deemed unconstitutional by the Supreme Court because it violated the Constitution's provisions for the separation of powers. However the concerns included in the NRA were later included in other laws, like the **NATIONAL LABOR RELATIONS ACT**, which maintained the basic structure and benefits of the NRA.

Public power commodities were created, like the **TENNESSEE VALLEY AUTHORITY**, under the New Deal. These existed to broadly manage not only power, but natural resources in the area. The Tennessee Valley Authority was federally funded with broad powers in the area to improve conditions, build dams, control fires, and even teach new agricultural methods to local farmers.

The **WORKS PROGRESS ADMINISTRATION** was designed to create job opportunities in public works projects of all types, including roads, schools, and airports. The **FEDERAL PROJECT NUMBER ONE** employed a number of writers, artists, and others on various projects, also designed to create jobs. The **CIVILIAN CONSERVATION CORPS**, made up of young men, worked on national and state park projects. These organizations got the unemployed off the streets and into jobs, providing new job skills and improving conditions for many in America.

The **FEDERAL DEPOSIT INSURANCE CORPORATION** was created to insure money stored in banks and to help people feel more confident about keeping their money in the bank. Today, the FDIC is commonly associated with banking, but it was newly created with the Banking Act of 1933, designed in response to the stock market crash of 1929 and Great Depression.

Perhaps the most significant change to American life established by the New Deal was the establishment of **SOCIAL SECURITY**. The Social Security Act of 1935 created the first insurance system to provide financial support for the elderly, disabled, widows, and surviving children. The initial act also created a means for funding Social Security payments. The existence of Social Security reduced poverty among the elderly and disabled; however, some jobs did not provide Social Security payments or coverage, particularly those worked by African-Americans.

The New Deal changed the political landscape of America. African-Americans were welcomed into some of the programs associated with the New Deal, largely as a result of the intervention of the First Lady, **ELEANOR ROOSEVELT**. Because of this, they began to vote largely Democratic, as did those involved in the labor and social welfare movements. This connection between Roosevelt's Democratic Party and the working classes continues even today.

Changing Technology and Culture

This was not just a period of political and economic change, but also technological and cultural change. By 1945, cars, buses, refrigerators, toasters, radios, and even airplanes had all become commonplace.

Many of the innovations of the nineteenth century became more common in this period, or were further developed. This includes the telephone, which soon became a feature of many American homes. Films provided not only entertainment, but also newsreels, and music came into homes with record players and radios. The radio also brought news into American homes across the country. In the home, labor saving devices appeared, including the refrigerator, the first electric washing machines, and the toaster. Over the course of this period, the horse and carriage were entirely replaced by a new form of transportation, the automobile. Buses and trains made travel across and around the United States easier than ever before. Bicycles also became more common, both in the cities and in rural areas. These new innovations also led to new ways of paying for things, as people now often bought goods on credit, allowing them to purchase things they could not have afforded before.

While changing technologies altered life in substantial and significant ways, they also increased the cleavages within society. Differences between rich and poor, white and African-American, and rural and urban became more clear, particularly as images and information about others became more available. Prior to the twentieth century, many people lived with relatively little access to information, save what came in the newspaper or through word-of-mouth. With the newsreels, films, and radio shows, that changed quickly. Now, people had a clear idea of what they didn't have, of what other lives looked like, and of what they might be missing. This new technology also created more shared experiences. For the first time, you didn't have to be physically present to hear a song played or see a theatrical production.

Culture changed just as rapidly during this period, especially in urban areas. This is the time of the **HARLEM RENAISSANCE**, when African-Americans created cultural forms and traditions that extended well beyond their own neighborhoods. The Harlem Renaissance began in 1918 and lasted into the 1930s. This movement included religion, literature, music, and visual arts, and remains one of the most influential cultural periods of the twentieth century.

DID YOU KNOW?
The poetry of Langston Hughes and music of Duke Ellington are closely associated with the Harlem Renaissance.

While the Harlem Renaissance incorporated nearly all aspects of culture, it was not the only significant development in this period. **JAZZ MUSIC**, and the dance and fashion associated with it, became popular, starting in the cities and spreading through the country. The flapper of the 1920s is closely associated with jazz, as is a new freedom for women, with bobbed hair and short dresses. Jazz incorporated both European and African-American musical traditions and developed over time, changing from Ragtime to the brass bands of the late 1930s.

In the visual arts, while Paris remained the art capital of the world, some American artists developed a distinctly American style, including Edward Hopper. Hopper painted American landscapes and interiors, as well as ordinary Americans, both in the city and countryside. These were people at work and play. Hopper was a realist, but did not affiliate himself with any artistic school or style. He remained active from the early twentieth century through the 1960s.

While motion pictures brought entertainment throughout the country, live theater remained prominent in major cities. This took different forms, from traditional plays to musical theater; however, there was also one particular form of theater exclusive to Jewish communities of Eastern European origin. Yiddish theater, performed by Ashkenazi Jews, became popular in New York City. Yiddish theater ranged from comedic to dramatic, and has, in recent years, become a subject of serious academic study. Yiddish theater in America reached its height in the 1920s, with shows of a scale and quality to rival those produced on Broadway.

American Expansionism

Between 1890 and the beginning of World War I in 1914, the United States gained political and diplomatic power in the world. The United States was interested in gaining land and territory, both in the Pacific and the Western Hemisphere during this time. The West had been won, leading to an end to internal expansionism of that sort. The motivations for expanding were largely economic and often involved both the government and private industry.

Spurred on by the yellow journalism of newspaper moguls Hearst and Pulitzer and the mysterious sinking of the *U.S.S. Maine* near Cuba, the United States undertook its first major foreign intervention—THE SPANISH-AMERICAN WAR—in 1898.

A young Teddy Roosevelt led a group of cavalry soldiers called the "Rough Riders" to help the Cuban people win independence from Spain. Winning the war gave America control of Puerto Rico, Guam, properties in the Caribbean, and parts of the Philippines.

At this time, the nation was politically divided. Some politicians favored imperialism, believing that extending American power would protect trade and provide additional economic security, while anti-imperialists questioned the costs of maintaining lands and a naval force to protect faraway interests.

Dollar diplomacy was President William Howard Taft's preferred foreign policy. This combination of public and private investment in foreign countries was used to further U.S. aims and support the development of democracy around the world.

The United States intervened on two occasions with the MEXICAN REVOLUTION, occupying Veracruz in 1914 and sending an expedition in to retaliate for violence in New Mexico in 1916 and 1917. U.S. actions supported the creation of a new Constitution in Mexico and the election of Venustiano Carraza.

World War I

World War I was a global war fought across many countries and continents from 1914 to 1918. Following the assassination of the Archduke of Austria-Hungary, Franz Ferdinand in June 1914, Europe entered the Great War, or what is now known as **WORLD WAR I**. By early August, every major European power was involved, but the United States remained neutral from 1914 through 1917. The United States did help to supply Britain during these years, and expressed progressive criticism over the use of German submarines to attack civilian vessels. The United States exerted diplomatic pressure to convince Germany to stop unrestricted submarine warfare at this time.

Gradually, public opinion changed, as did President Woodrow Wilson's. Following the 1915 German submarine attack on a British ship, the *Lusitania*, which held 128 American passengers, the United States began preparing for war.

In January 1917, the Germans resumed submarine warfare. Initially the United States responded by arming merchant ships to fight back, but did not directly participate. The British soon intercepted a German telegram promising Mexico financial support if it would declare war on the United States.

Though Mexico remained neutral in the conflict, this telegram, known as the **ZIMMERMAN TELEGRAM**, enraged the American people and caused the United States to officially enter World War I in April 1917.

By the spring of 1918, America had set up the Selective Service, or the **DRAFT**, and was shipping 10,000 fresh soldiers to the battlefields of France each day. On the home front, women went to work, propaganda supported the war effort, and everyone worked to make do at home to help the soldiers, from growing their own food in backyard gardens, to knitting socks for the soldiers. The new American forces provided the support and morale needed to achieve an Allied victory.

U.S. **PRESIDENT WOODROW WILSON** was a key figure in determining the terms of peace, originating in his **FOURTEEN POINTS** speech made in January 1918. Wilson's goals included the creation of the **LEAGUE OF NATIONS**, a precursor to today's United Nations.

The United States did not sign the **TREATY OF VERSAILLES**, which ended World War I, or join the League of Nations, but it did make peace through individual treaties with warring nations. Wilson was unable to secure the support of the Senate for involvement in the League of Nations, weakening the organization as a whole.

After World War I, the United States returned to a policy of isolationism, this time augmented with a new status as a diplomatic and military power. Many in the United States saw casualties as unreasonably high for the benefits gained from intervention in World War I. While the U.S. Senate, in particular, favored non-interventionist politics, the ability to intervene was maintained through military strength. Intervention did occur in Latin America, along with broad support for democracy in these closer nations. Isolationism applied primarily to Europe and Asia. The isolationist policy continued throughout the 1920s and 1930s, becoming stronger and more dominant during the Great Depression.

President William Harding led the **Washington Arms Conference** in 1921 and 1922. Several European and East Asian powers signed treaties agreeing to limit the size of their navies. This led to the growth of Japan as a power in East Asia.

The **Stimson Doctrine**, crafted in response to the 1931 invasion of Manchuria by Japan, stated that the United States would not recognize border or territory changes executed by military force. This was a diplomatic action, but one not backed by military or economic force.

The **Neutrality Acts** of the 1930s reflected the isolationism of the period. These Acts were designed specifically to address the U.S. role in global political and military conflicts. In 1935, with war looming, the First Neutrality Act prohibited the sale of weapons or arms to foreign nations, as well as loans to foreign nations at war. The Second Neutrality Act banned American shippers from transporting arms and Americans from taking passage on ships of belligerent nations. The export embargo now not only included arms, but all goods; however, belligerent nations could acquire non-military goods from the United States by purchasing them, paying for them, and leaving with them on non-American ships. The final Neutrality Act of 1939 extended this cash-and-carry policy to arms, allowing the United States to support the efforts of Britain and France in World War II. These Acts were invalidated by the entry of the United States into World War II in 1941.

The Roaring Twenties

The 1920s were the era of jazz, the **FLAPPER**, and Prohibition. It was a glamourous time, and for many in the United States, a very successful one. Many people invested in the stock market during this period.

This decade saw glimmers of the present-day postmodern zeitgeist in America, particularly in late modern art, literature, and philosophy. **Postmodernism** is characterized by a major distrust for authority, ideology, and over-arching theories, and resists concrete definitions of creative expression. Though postmodernism was still "late modernism" and incubating in the *avant-garde* of European thought in those days, and would not emerge as a major theme in America until the 1960s, its casual iconoclasm and anti-authoritarianism was also developing in American culture

DID YOU KNOW?

Some examples of late modernists that laid the foundations for postmodernism in this time period include Gertrude Stein, Pablo Picasso, Ernest Hemingway, and F. Scott Fitzgerald.

One notable symbol of the 1920s was the flapper girl: A woman who flouted social conventions and traditional cultural mores by drinking alcohol at illegal speakeasies, wearing short skirts, listening to jazz music, smoking cigarettes in public, and carrying an attitude of general disdain for tradition.

The Roaring Twenties came crashing to a dramatic end in September 1929, when stock prices began to rapidly fall. The resultant panic culminated in the Wall Street Crash of 1929, also known as Black Tuesday. This heralded the beginning of the GREAT DEPRESSION.

After the fall of the stock market, the economy crumbled. The wealthy lost their fortunes, businesses closed their doors, and ordinary people lost their life savings as banks collapsed. Unemployment rose to roughly twenty-five percent in the United States. The Great Depression impacted all levels of society, from the richest to the poorest.

The Great Depression began during Herbert Hoover's presidency; however, he failed to take action to help the American people. In fact, as homelessness increased, shantytowns made of cardboard and tarpaper sprang up, commonly called "Hoovervilles." With the election of Franklin D. Roosevelt in 1933, the United States began to climb out of the Great Depression, but the nation remained in an economic recession until the beginning of World War II. The economic output required for the war altered the U.S. economy significantly.

In overseeing both the recovery from the Depression and World War II, Franklin Roosevelt became the only president to serve more than two terms, which had been an unofficial rule for previous presidents, based on George Washington's decision to serve only two terms. After FDR's unprecedented four terms as president, which earned him the moniker, "The King of America," the twenty-second amendment was passed in 1951, limiting future presidencies to two terms.

World War II

The United States took steps to support Britain and France in World War II and to object to Japanese actions in the invasion of Manchuria. The United States became progressively more concerned about the war in Europe as democracies fell, with Germany occupying France in June 1940. In March 1941, the Lend-Lease Act specifically offered support to Britain, including military support for ships transporting arms and goods. War production increased in the United States from 1940 onward.

The United States entered the war on December 6, 1941, when the Japanese bombed the U.S. naval base at Pearl Harbor in Hawaii. Prior to the attack on Pearl Harbor, most Americans were unwilling to become involved.

Adolf Hitler declared war on the United States days later. On January 1, 1942, twenty-six nations joined together, agreeing not to make individual peace agreements with the AXIS POWERS, forming a group now known as the ALLIED FORCES, or Allies.

Within the Allied Forces, U.S. President Roosevelt, British Prime Minister WINSTON CHURCHILL, and Secretary JOSEF STALIN of the Soviet Union became known as THE BIG THREE.

The United States began to mobilize troops, arms, and supplies. Unemployment fell and many new workers entered the workforce to take the place of men gone to war. Production increased to meet the needs for arms, vehicles, planes, uniformsm and other goods. U.S. involvement was an essential factor in stopping Hitler's forces in Germany, and the growth of the Japanese Empire. The United States brought arms, supplies, and, most importantly, soldiers when it entered the war on both fronts. At home, people pulled together to scrimp for the war effort, help soldiers, and participate in their patriotic duty.

The war brought improved opportunities and rights for women and, eventually, African-Americans, but also resulted in major civil rights violations in the United States. Until 1941, the U.S. military remained fully segregated. African-Americans were frequently denied positions of authority. In response, African-American soldiers began the **DOUBLE V CAMPAIGN**, calling for not only victory for America, but military desegregation.

African-American units played key roles in the war, including the heroic actions of the **TUSKEGEE AIRMEN** in North Africa and Italy. Military desegregation did not occur until 1948.

World War II inspired a number of technological advancements on both sides. Air campaigns were key to the war effort, along with new technology like sonar, used to identify submarines. Medical advancements were also a result of the war; however, the most significant technological advancement of the war years in America was the **ATOM BOMB.**

Work on an atom bomb began in Germany in 1939, when scientists first split the uranium atom. Scientists living in the United States, including the German Albert Einstein and Italian Enrico Fermi, notified President Roosevelt of this finding and the risks it posed. Roosevelt did not want to build an atomic weapon, but he allowed the **MANHATTAN PROJECT** to go forward. In December 1942, nuclear facilities around the nation—including a large one in Los Alamos, New Mexico led by Robert Oppenheimer—began work on developing the bomb. Many who worked on the Manhattan Project were unaware of what they were developing. The first bomb test took place on July 16, 1945.

On August 6, 1945, the United States dropped an atomic bomb, called "Little Boy" on the city of Hiroshima. A second bomb, "Fat Man," was dropped on the city of Nagasaki on August 9. These ended the war with Japan, but took 200,000 civilian lives.

World War II was fought in Europe as well as in the Pacific. American troops invaded occupied France in June 1944 and pushed east to Berlin, arriving at the same time as the Soviet Red Army and defeating Germany once and for all.

The actions of the American military brought the war to an end, and America would have a strong voice in international relations moving forward. World War II ended at the **Paris Peace Treaties of 1947**. After the war, Secretary of State George Marshall proposed **the Marshall Plan**, a $17 billion program ($160 billion in today's dollars,) to help rebuild Europe.

Many former imperial possessions of various nations gained their freedom after the war, and the United States prepared to help rebuild the world, including Germany and Japan. Part of that process was ensuring that those who committed war crimes came to justice.

In 1945 and 1946, the United States led Allied military tribunals that investigated and sentenced Nazi war criminals to death. Journalist Edward R. Murrow's radio broadcasts on the **Nuremberg Trials** brought home the reality of the Holocaust to millions of Americans.

As World War II ended, a new enemy grew stronger: the Soviet Union.

CHAPTER EIGHT
The Cold War and the Civil Rights Movement
1945–1980

The United States and the Soviet Union were allies in World War II, working together to defeat Germany. It was the Soviets who first reached Berlin, taking the city with the support of U.S. bombers. Control of Europe was divided at the end of the war, with specific spheres of influence splitting east and west. By the end of the war, the Soviets controlled all of Eastern Europe and much of Central Europe. Almost at once, the Soviets began exerting additional political control over these regions, called the **EASTERN BLOC**.

In 1947, President Truman adopted a policy of **CONTAINMENT** to prevent the spread of communism. During this period, Truman established the **CENTRAL INTELLIGENCE AGENCY**, or **CIA**.

At the end of the war, the Allies decided that Germany would be divided through the city of Berlin, with the eastern half controlled by the Soviet Union. In 1947, the United States enacted the Marshall Plan, providing significant economic aid to Western Europe, including Germany. The Soviets disallowed countries in the Eastern Bloc from accepting U.S. aid. In June 1948, the Soviets stopped allowing U.S. vehicles to supply the western-controlled half of Berlin. The United States and its allies began air drops to supply the city with food and other essentials. In 1949, Stalin proposed to unite Germany, but without allowing any alliances or aid from Western democracies. The remaining Allies refused. In April 1949, the Western powers united to form the **NORTH ATLANTIC TREATY ORGANIZATION** or **NATO** and combined their zones of control in Germany to create West Germany. NATO was designed to help protect democracy, both in Europe and abroad.

The **COLD WAR** intensified when the Soviet Union tested its first nuclear bombs, creating an arms race that would continue throughout this period. The arms race included not only the atomic bomb, but later the development of the **HYDROGEN BOMB**, and the space race, with the United States and the Soviet Union each seeking to outdo the other. The hydrogen bomb or nuclear, rather than atomic bomb, is approximately fifty times more powerful than the bombs dropped on Hiroshima and Nagasaki at the end of World War II. Both the United States and the Soviet Union were prepared to use devastating technology, including nuclear bombs, in the face of any attack. This strategy was called massive retaliation and was designed to prevent any acts of aggression.

Conditions during the Cold War varied. There were periods of *détente*, or relative calm, with little action from either side, as well as periods of increased tension when war seemed imminent and the need to prepare for war was crucial. The United States maintained a substantial military presence, both at home and abroad, to address the communist threat. Other key moments in the Cold War included a meeting of U.S. **PRESIDENT JOHN F. KENNEDY** and Soviet leader **NIKITA KHRUSHCHEV** in 1961, along the building of the Berlin Wall dividing East and West Berlin in the same year.

DID YOU KNOW?
The U.S. conflict with the Soviets peaked in 1962 with the Bay of Pigs; after this incident, the two countries never again came so close to the brink of open war.

The containment policies of the Cold War did not just impact Europe. These policies were applied internationally to reduce the spread of communism, particularly after the Communist Revolution in China. They were also applied in Latin America, where the United States supported governments that opposed communism. In some cases, these governments were not burgeoning democracies, but dictatorships guilty of significant human rights abuses. President Kennedy's Good Neighbor plan was well-intentioned, but the decades did not bear out the success of this strategy.

Korea

The **KOREAN WAR** began as a conflict between North and South Korea. At the end of the war, as in Germany, the Soviets and United States divided Korea. The North half of Korea was under Soviet control and eventually, contrary to the agreement with the West, became a communist state. South Korea, with support from the West, would become a democracy. The two halves of the divided nation soon clashed.

In 1950, the United Nations supported assisting South Korea while China offered aid to communist North Korea. The United States, alongside UN troops, entered the Korean War.

The Korean War ended in a stalemate in 1954, with both sides agreeing to an armistice. The Korean War did not reunite the country, but led to the maintenance of a demilitarized zone between the two nations ever since, and served to protect Japan from a potential Chinese communist incursion, and illustrated the willingness of the United States to apply containment policies in Asia. The United States retains a military presence in South Korea today.

Vietnam

The conflict in Vietnam is, in many ways, similar to the Korean War. American military advisors became involved in 1950, with American troop involvement throughout the 1960s. The country was divided into North and South Vietnam. The communist North fought the South, which was supported by the United States and other democratic allies. South Vietnamese and allied troops fought both the **Viet Cong**, a guerilla communist group headquartered in the South, and the North Vietnamese Army. A peace treaty was signed in 1973; most American troops left the country, but this did not end the war.

In April 1975, the South Vietnamese capital city of Saigon fell to North Vietnamese forces, prompting a hasty U.S. evacuation of its personnel, along with tens of thousands of south Vietnamese people.

The war took a great toll on human lives, both Vietnamese and American, and led to an anti-war movement that made up the primary political component of the 1960s counterculture in America. Both Vietnam and Korea represent failures in the U.S. policy of containment during the Cold War.

Intervention in Africa and the Middle East

The process of international decolonization following World War II led to a number of government changes in Africa and the Middle East. Independent governments were newly established, many without a clear political ideology. Both the United States and Soviet Union wanted to ally themselves with these countries to expand their respective spheres of influence. Furthermore, the Middle East had a valuable commodity, much in need in the United States—oil.

In 1956, the United States played a pivotal role in forcing Britain and France to support the Israeli invasion of Egypt during the Suez Crisis. This became critical after the **Arab Oil Embargo** and **Energy Crisis** in 1973.

The Embargo and Crisis were the result of U.S. support for Israel following a series of attacks on Israel by Syria and Egypt. In 1974, the United States formed the **International Energy Agency (IEA)** in an attempt to control the efforts of the **Organization of the Petroleum Exporting Countries (OPEC)**. While these measures were practical, others had a more lasting negative impact.

The Civil Rights Movement

While significant social welfare programs were in place prior to World War II, many of the programs still in use today were created in the second half of the twentieth century. Also, significant steps were taken for rights for African-Americans and other minorities, as well as women. Many brave individuals were involved in these fights, particularly for civil rights for African-Americans.

The first steps toward comprehensive change in civil rights came during World War II, as defense contractors were banned from racist hiring policies. This was followed by the desegregation of the Armed Forces in 1948, both by Executive Act. Nonetheless, **Jim Crow laws** remained common in the South, and racism was prevalent throughout the United States. Jim Crow laws segregated schools, hospitals, buses, lunch counters, and other facilities.

School segregation ended with a judicial decision of the U.S. Supreme Court, *Brown v. Board of Education of Topeka*. The process of school desegregation was not easy, and eventually, the National Guard was called in to help support African-American students attending white schools.

Equally damaging were voting restrictions that kept African-American voters from the polls. These ranged from legal measures, like poll taxes and literacy tests, to illegal ones, like threats of violence.

In 1964, the **Civil Rights Act** outlawed discrimination on the basis of race, color, religion, sex, or national origin. It also provided for desegregation and federal elections monitoring. The twenty-fourth amendment also passed, outlawing poll taxes in federal elections.

Over time, the federal government's power to enforce civil rights legislation increased, but there were eventually conflicts within the civil rights movement, particularly between those who advocated non-violence and those willing to consider a violent response to discrimination, such as the **Black Panthers**.

Those who fought for civil rights were men and women from all racial backgrounds. They included both well-educated and less-educated people, and people from all economic classes. Many were driven by strong religious convictions, believing devoutly in the righteousness of their cause.

Dr. Martin Luther King Jr. was a pastor and leader in the civil rights movement who gained national prominence with his organization of the Montgomery, AL bus boycott in the wake of activist **Rosa Parks**' arrest.

King supported non-violent resistance and served as a key figure in the movement, providing a voice for many that reached politicians in Washington D.C. King was a remarkable orator, and the recipient of the 1964 Nobel Peace Prize. Assassinated in 1968, King is remembered with a U.S. federal holiday each year.

FANNIE LOU HAMER began her work as a civil rights activist in the early 1960s, working to register African-Americans in Mississippi to vote. On her first trip by bus, she became known as the "lady who sang the hymns" and was recruited to fill a broader role in the voter registration movement. In 1964, she spoke about civil rights at the Democratic National Convention and many across America watched her speech on television. Hamer went on to run for Congress twice and work for the development of Head Start and other programs.

Congressman JOHN LEWIS is an African-American who came of age in the early years of the civil rights movement. As a young man, he joined the FREEDOM RIDERS to encourage voter registration. By the age of twenty-three, he was recognized as a leader of the movement. He remained active in the civil rights movement, eventually taking political office, first in the city of Atlanta. In 1986, Lewis was elected to represent Georgia's Fifth Congressional District, and still serves in the House today.

As the chief litigator in *Brown v. Board of Education*, Thurgood Marshall made a name for himself as a voice for civil rights. He went on to become the U.S. Solicitor General, then the first African-American to sit on the Supreme Court. His judicial voice was key in a number of decisions on civil rights and criminal procedures until his retirement in 1991.

While the initial fight for civil rights involved African-Americans, the Civil Rights Act of 1964 provided broader protections to various groups, including women.

The FEMINIST MOVEMENT grew throughout the 1960s and 1970s, with the publication of books like BETTY FRIEDAN's *The Feminine Mystique* and the work of activist GLORIA STEINEM, who founded *Ms. Magazine*.

Women worked for the passage of a constitutional amendment guaranteeing equal rights, but it was never successfully ratified. In more recent years, some states have passed legislation protecting the rights of gay, lesbian, and transgender individuals. Work continues for civil rights for all minority groups of Americans.

The Great Society

As awareness of civil rights issues grew, so too did an awareness of poverty in America, as well as the weaknesses in the public sector. In 1958, John Galbraith wrote *The Affluent Society*. According to Galbraith, private industry was growing wealthier in America, while the public sector was becoming poorer. This was increasing the gap between rich and poor. Galbraith's work influenced later social policy.

In 1960, President Kennedy used the term *New Frontier* in his presidential acceptance speech, which became a label for his social and domestic policies aimed at reducing poverty and infrastructure investment.

After President Kennedy was assassinated in Dallas, Texas in November, 1963, **LYNDON B. JOHNSON** assumed the presidency and launched a large series of social programs, which he called the **GREAT SOCIETY**, to reduce poverty and hunger in America. Johnson's programs had broad legislative support, with eighty-four of eighty-seven passed into law.

These included the Civil Rights Act, the Voting Rights Act, as well as the creation of the National Endowment for the Humanities, Job Corps, the Department of Transportation, the Department of Housing and Urban Development, and expansions to Social Security that created Medicare and Medicaid.

The **VOTING RIGHTS ACT** allowed the federal government to provide support for and enforce voters' rights, including an end to individual states' restrictive measures.

Immigration laws were reformed in 1965 with the Immigration and Nationality Act. It addressed the needs of specific immigrant and refugee communities, including Cubans and Filipinos, gave foreign nationals a "pathway to citizenship," and did away with quotas, allowing more people from around the world to move to America in search of opportunity.

These new attitudes extended beyond Johnson's Great Society. In the Supreme Court, cases supporting individual rights changed how Americans view the law. *Griswold v. Connecticut* supported privacy rights, particularly in regard to married couples and contraception; however, the decision has been applied more broadly. The *Miranda v. Arizona* decision specified the terms of police procedure and required that police notify suspects of their rights; these are now called **MIRANDA RIGHTS**.

Later in this period, an interest in the well-being of the planet's environment grew. Some of these values were shared with traditional conservationists, but others were more significantly concerned with the damage done by private businesses, including large-scale agriculture. Writer and activist Rachel Carson, author of *Silent Spring*, helped to redefine the environmental movement in the modern world, building on the work of great American conservationists throughout history, such as Thomas Jefferson, Henry David Thoreau, Teddy Roosevelt, and more. In terms of public policy, industrial pollution was the most significant concern in this period. The Clean Air Act of 1970 set limits on industrial emissions for the first time.

Many of these actions were quite liberal, as they used public policy and government regulation to achieve social change. The large number of liberal reforms passed combined with a strong counterculture movement led to a conservative backlash. Conservative groups questioned and objected to governmental social engineering, preferring that social welfare remain part of the private sphere. Conservatives focused on traditional religious and societal values; though there were many that resisted civil rights legislation and laws pertaining to women's rights, they were not necessarily racist or sexist. Many desired a more just society for all, but wanted the American people to end injustice in an organic fashion, without governmental regulation (and the subsequent empowerment of the public sphere.)

The Nixon Presidency

The conservative rebound included both religious and political organizations. Americans elected Republican **RICHARD NIXON** to the presidency in 1968 with a commanding mandate—he carried over 300 electoral votes and more than two-thirds of states. Nixon went on to implement many conservative goals of the time, including tamping down spiraling inflation, transferring powers from the federal government to the states, and launching the **WAR ON DRUGS**. Some of his more controversial, but lasting, changes to American policy included establishing the **ENVIRONMENTAL PROTECTION AGENCY**, successfully desegregating federal public schools, and enacting the first federal affirmative action programs.

Nixon's most significant accomplishment may have been ending the divisive Vietnam War. He implemented a policy of Vietnamization—training the South Vietnamese to fight in place of American troops.

Despite significant accomplishments, Nixon's presidency was dogged by repeated scandal. First, Vice-President Spiro Agnew was forced to resign after indictment on tax evasion and bribery charges; both crimes took place while he was governor of Maryland.

The **WATERGATE SCANDAL** derailed Nixon's second term. The Watergate was a hotel where the Democratic National Committee had its headquarters; after two reporters, Woodward and Bernstein, found Nixon to be complicit with a 1972 break-in, he resigned—the first president in U.S. history to do so.

Conservative groups went on to challenge some of Nixon's legacy, including affirmative action. The *Regents of the University of California v. Bakke* case in 1978 brought the Supreme Court into a fight over the legality of using race as college admission criteria. Opponents argued that affirmative action violated the Equal Protection Clause of the fourteenth amendment, but the Supreme Court ultimately disagreed.

Cultural Changes

When World War II ended, young men returned home, ready to buy homes and start families. Assistance programs for veterans helped with these goals, and this resulted in a *baby boom*—a large spike in the American population. Today, the people born between 1946 and 1964 are known as "the Baby Boom Generation," **BABY BOOMERS** or simply "Boomers."

Women removed themselves from the work force, after taking a dominant role for several years, and returned to the home. This return wasn't always a happy one, and many women struggled to adapt.

Families enjoyed more technological advances than ever before, as new gadgets made home life easier. The car became a dominant feature of American culture, particularly as families left the cities for suburban communities. The population of the Sun Belt, or the southern United States from the East Coast to the West Coast, grew dramatically, as people moved into warmer regions, bought homes, and made lives there. Jobs were abundant and people were united, both through the shared experience of World War II and through their distaste for the new enemy: the Soviet Union.

In the 1950s, CONSUMERISM was viewed as a patriotic duty. More affluent members of society felt social pressure to "keep up with the Joneses," which meant buying ever more and newer high-priced goods to compete with their neighbors' affluence.

While American society greatly valued conformity in the years after the war, hints at the great cultural changes of the 1960s could be seen in the preceding decade. A new youth culture, centered on rock 'n roll music was beginning, as young people went to dances, listened to their own music, and eagerly bought record albums.

At the same time, the Beats, or BEATNIKS, who included figures such as Allan Ginsberg, William S. Burroughs, and Jack Kerouac, took part in the "San Francisco Renaissance," which led to the "hippie" movement many years later and defined counterculture for decades to come.

The Beatniks blatantly rejected traditional American values, rebelled against social norms, and favored free sexuality, drug us,e and personal expression.

Counterculture in the 1960s was far more political than the Beat Generation had been, galvanized by opposition to the Vietnam War. The hippies were a youth culture, driven by individuals in their late teens, many of whom gathered in San Francisco and other urban areas. They refused many of the traditional trappings of society, including jobs and marriage, and created their own subculture. This continued through the 1970s, and their cultural influence is still prevalent in America today.

CHAPTER NINE
The Turn of the Millennium
1980–present

The liberalism of the 1960s and relative chaos of the 1970s was followed by another conservative backlash in the 1980s. Confidence in the government fell dramatically through the 1970s for several reasons. Scandals like Watergate, the economic pain of the OPEC Oil Embargo, and the failure of the Vietnam War contributed, as did dramatic inflation.

Democrat Jimmy Carter's presidency was marred by multiple blunders. Though he improved relations with the Soviet Union, he presided over multiple foreign policy failures.

The Iranian Hostage Crisis led to worries throughout the United States. During the 1970s, the United States supported the reign of the Shah of Iran, who welcomed Western influences. In the late 1970s, a religious revolution took place, and in the midst of this, fifty-two Americans were taken hostage for nearly a year and a half. Eventual negotiations after the beginning of the Iran-Iraq War led to their release, however only after a failed military action ordered by President Carter. These troubles combined to create an environment that supported change; once again, the American people handed a commanding presidential mandate to a conservative movement figure, RONALD REAGAN.

Reagan was a transformative figure in American politics. Since his presidency, when he declared that "the era of big government is over," some of America's most hotly contested political fights have been over the size, role, and efficacy of the federal government.

Reagan's changes were numerous, including ending the Cold War, dramatically reducing taxes, widespread deregulation of American industry, revitalizing the political power of American conservatism, battling labor unions head-on, and drastically increasing military spending in the defense budget. Reagan

DID YOU KNOW?
President Reagan survived an assassination attempt in 1981.

appointed three Justices to the Supreme Court, though his selection of Robert Bork was blocked in the Senate.

In 1988, Reagan passed the CIVIL LIBERTIES ACT OF **1988**, which authorized $20,000 in reparations to every Japanese-American interned during World War II for a total of $1.2 billion. It also included a formal apology on behalf of the United States.

In 1994, the Republican Party relied upon the Reagan model for the 1994 Contract with America created by Speaker of the House Newt Gingrich. Their goals included a balanced budget, welfare reform, a child tax credit, and the imposition of term limits. One of the few significant social successes for conservatives was the *Planned Parenthood v. Casey* decision. While this did reaffirm a constitutional right to abortion, it allowed some limitations in the state of Pennsylvania, including parental consent, to stand as constitutional and not an undue burden. Though conservative goals included smaller government, reduced spending, and changes to social welfare legislation, Medicare and Medicaid both expanded throughout the Reagan era, and the budget deficit exploded to historically unprecedented proportions.

Polarizing conflicts between liberals and conservatives have continued throughout both Republican and Democratic presidencies and Congresses since 1980.

The Culture War

The period between 1980 and the present saw tectonic changes to America's social fabric. Conservatives and liberals have bitterly fought a culture war throughout the last thirty-five years.

Evangelical religious organizations began to grow in size and prominence from the 1980s onward, and the conservative movement became increasingly linked with these organizations.

The MORAL MAJORITY, founded in 1979, remained active throughout the 1980s. This organization helped to politicize evangelical Christians, encouraging their involvement in government and creating a clear image of a liberal threat to traditional values.

Another non-profit, FOCUS ON THE FAMILY, formed in 1977. Focus on the Family's daily broadcast of Dr. James Dobson's radio show began in 1980 to a large audience. By the early 1980s, this organization had gained substantial political clout, with Dobson serving on political advisory committees. Today, evangelical organizations are still closely associated with conservative politicians and movement conservative organizations, such as those affiliated with the Tea Party.

A notable liberal defeat in this period was the high-profile saga of the Equal Rights Amendment (ERA) that guaranteed equality to women. First drafted in 1923, feminists such as Gloria Steinem of the National Organization for Women strongly advocated for it in the 1970s and 1980s. The proposed text of the ERA reads as such:

- ▶ Section One: Equality of rights under the law shall not be denied or abridged by the United States or by any State on account of sex.

- ▶ Section Two: Congress shall have the power to enforce, by appropriate legislation, the provisions of this article.

- ▶ Section Three: This amendment shall take effect two years after the date of ratification.

By 1977, the ERA had passed both houses of Congress, and had been ratified by thirty-five of the required thirty-eight states, but ultimately met a Congressionally-imposed deadline first in 1978 and then again in 1982 without receiving the required ratifications.

One of the strongest opponents of the ERA was **Phyllis Schlafly**, a conservative activist who argued for traditional gender roles through her organization, the Eagle Forum, which she founded in 1972.

In the 1990s, the battlegrounds of the culture war took place in the media—particularly the television and film industries. Both conservative groups and liberal politicians like Senators Al Gore and Joseph Lieberman railed against the perceived immorality of film and television, and fought for legislation establishing parental controls in electronics (widely remembered as the V-Chip Law.)

In 2004, President George W. Bush proposed an amendment to the Constitution that would have defined marriage as between one man and one woman. This was in response to a growing social movement—this time led by conservative activists and writers such as Evan Wolfson and Andrew Sullican – pushing for the expansion of marriage rights to gay and lesbian Americans. The amendment gained little traction, and American public opinion drastically changed on the subject in just eleven years—in 2015, the Supreme Court struck down all bans on same-sex marriage with the landmark case *Obergefell v. Hodges*.

Additionally, legislation and judicial decisions have led to increased rights for gays and lesbian Americans. Prior to the 1990s, if service members were found to be homosexual while serving in the armed forces, they were subject to immediate discharge, often under other than honorable conditions or for bad conduct, which stripped them of their rights to veterans' services. Under President Bill Clinton, an executive order, commonly called **Don't Ask, Don't Tell**, was put into place. This allowed closeted individuals to serve, but did not allow service members to be "open" about their sexual orientation. Don't Ask, Don't Tell was repealed in 2011, allowing gays and lesbians to openly serve.

In 2008, with the country embroiled in two costly and controversial wars in Iraq and Afghanistan, and facing the worst financial crisis since the Great Depression, Americans elected **Barack Obama** to the White House—the first black president in history.

The Cold War Ends

By the late 1970s, the Cold War settled into a relatively calm state, however, this calm period relied upon the doctrine of massive retaliation, also known as "mutually assured destruction." When President Reagan was elected, defense spending increased significantly as he focused on increasing the technological capability of the military.

The largest investment of the early 1980s was the **STAR WARS**, or the Strategic Defense Initiative missile defense system, which was designed to bring an end to the policy of massive retaliation. The hope was to be able to shoot missiles down from space.

Over time, Reagan developed a good working relationship with the Soviet leader, Mikhail Gorbachev, and eventually negotiated the creation of a mutual arms treaty, called START I. Though the glimmers of peace were visible, both the Soviets and the United States continued to increase their nuclear arsenals.

Late in the 1980s, the Soviet Union began to fail as a state, bankrupted by their need to keep up with American defense spending and bereft of support from satellite countries that increasingly embraced democracy and American values. The Berlin Wall fell in 1989, and in 1991, the Soviet Union collapsed. After the collapse, both the American and Russian people were able to agree to the START I treaty, and begin the process of reducing their Cold War nuclear arsenals. Throughout the 1990s and the first decade of the twenty-first century, conditions between Russia and the United States remained relatively friendly, though the first hint of renewed tensions came during the first presidency of Vladimir Putin, between 2000 and 2008. Since 2014, U.S.-Russia relations have worsened significantly.

The collapse of the Soviet Union also changed the position of the United States in the world. As the now disjoined countries of the Soviet Union were either independent or only loosely organized into the Russian Federation, the United States emerged as the most dominant and most significant global power in the world.

The Gulf War and the War on Terror

While the United States was involved in a Middle Eastern conflict in the early 1990s called **OPERATION DESERT STORM**, life in the United States was relatively peaceful.

The Cold War ended and there were no significant threats on the horizon. However on September 11, 2001, everything changed. Nineteen terrorists trained in Afghanistan hijacked planes and flew them into the World Trade Center in New York and the Pentagon in Washington, D.C, infamously known as **9/11**. This was the first attack on U.S. soil since the bombing of Pearl Harbor in World War II.

DID YOU KNOW?
Desert Storm was the first war to be broadcast live into Americans' homes via 24/7 cable news coverage.

The United States responded by invading Afghanistan and deposing the ruling faction there, called the **TALIBAN**. Two years later, President George W. Bush ordered U.S. troops into Iraq to depose its leader, Saddam Hussein.

There has been a great deal of controversy surrounding American involvement in both countries throughout the global War on Terror. The war in Iraq was based on the U.S. assertion that Saddam Hussein had a large-scale program of chemical weapons, and was attempting to build a nuclear bomb—both known as "weapons of mass destruction." After eight years of war, no such weapons were ever found.

A large number of individuals have also been imprisoned indefinitely and without trial in U.S. prisons on foreign soil, including at Abu Ghraib and Guantanamo Bay, where U.S. personnel have tortured and humiliated prisoners.

After 9/11, Congress passed a number of laws that enhanced the government's ability to search, intercept, and prosecute acts of terror. The most notable was the **PATRIOT ACT**, which vastly increased the government's surveillance capabilities.

Other measures in the wake of 9/11 include the establishment of the **DEPARTMENT OF HOMELAND SECURITY** and the expansion of the National Security Agency's powers and mandate. Many infringements upon Americans' rights to privacy have occurred since then, including government monitoring of phone and internet transmissions, government monitoring of individual spending activity, and additional screening in airports.

Economic Change

Between the 1950s and the 1970s, America was home to a thriving industrial community. There were many union jobs available, with good wages and benefits, even for individuals without job training. With hard work, many people could work at the same job throughout their lives and retire with pensions. Home ownership and personal betterment were within reach. This changed in the 1980s. Fiscal conservatives did not support workers' unions and many companies, encouraged by free market practices, moved their industrial operations overseas.

This trend became even more dominant after President Bill Clinton (a Democrat) signed the **NORTH AMERICAN FREE TRADE AGREEMENT** or **NAFTA** in 1994. Though opponents argued that it would cause America to lose thousands of manufacturing jobs, NAFTA still passed, allowing many employers to move their companies to Mexico in search of less expensive labor. This resulted in lower illegal immigration to the United States, but wages for American workers stagnated.

The changing economy of America led to a number of political debates on topics like free trade, social welfare, and banking in America. Broadly speaking, perspectives on this fell along party lines.

> ▶ Democrats favored increased spending and social welfare programs, including health care, Social Security, Medicare, and Medicaid. Aid for

corporations was less popular, and banking reforms favored increased, rather than decreased regulation.

▶ Republicans favored a balanced budget, lower taxes, and decreased spending. In particular, Republicans fought against social welfare spending, including anti-poverty programs and government health care reform, preferring non-governmental, market-driven solutions to social ills. Corporate-aid programs are generally well-accepted among Republicans, along with decreased corporate and banking regulation.

Current discussions concerning the economy have focused on deficit reduction, job creation, inflation, and health care reform. Economic issues are particularly controversial in today's politics.

Environmental issues have grown in importance since 1980, with significant debates over the welfare of the planet. Climate change, pollution, and the use of fossil fuels are all critical issues in the modern world. The use of fossil fuels is further complicated by difficult relations with the Middle East, a major supplier of oil. This has led to frequent discussion and conflict over U.S. oil drilling and American demand for other resources, such as natural gas.

DID YOU KNOW?
The scientific community overwhelmingly agrees that global warming poses a major threat to the planet, most notably by the threat of melting ice caps and flooded coastal areas. However many politicians continue to claim that global warming is a hoax.

The world economy was also revolutionized in this time period by the commercialization of the Internet. Initially conceived in a military research lab, by the year 1999, the Internet brought entertainment, shopping, business, research, and much more into American's homes.

In 2010, President Obama signed into law the **PATIENT PRO-TECTION AND AFFORDABLE CARE ACT**, which came to be known as "Obamacare." The controversial bill guaranteed health insurance coverage to millions of uninsured Americans. It also imposed a health insurance mandate that conservatives bitterly fought, and despite repeated guarantees from President Obama to the contrary, also forced millions of Americans to change their primary care physicians.

The Clinton Presidency

In 1992, the American people elected a Democrat, **BILL CLINTON**, to the White House. Clinton was an ambitious president who sought to institute many domestic reforms, but his failed attempt at nationalized health care galvanized conservative opposition and ultimately handed control of both houses of Congress to his Republican opponents.

Clinton served two terms as President, and his legacy includes the implementation of "Don't Ask, Don't Tell," the passage of NAFTA, the passage of the federal Defense of Marriage Act, which prevented the federal government from recognizing non-heterosexual marriage, the Family Leave and Medical Act, which expanded leave provisions for workers, and SCHIP, which provided healthcare for millions of children.

Clinton's presidency was also marked by a significant number of scandals and controversies, notably in the arenas of campaign finance, presidential pardons, the Whitewater real estate deal ,and his extramarital affair with a White House intern, Monica Lewinsky.

In connection with a Republican-led investigation into the Lewinsky affair, Clinton was tried and impeached by the House of Representatives for perjury and obstruction of justice—the first president to have been impeached by the House since Andrew Johnson in 1868. Like Johnson, Clinton was acquitted by the Senate, and served the remainder of his second term in the White House.

According to the Constitution, if a federal officer is impeached, they are subject to the following repercussions: They can undergo impeachment proceedings, be tried in court for a related crime, and if found guilty, be removed from office and banned from holding office in the future.

Shifting Demographics

Demographic changes in the U.S. population have altered the culture of the United States in recent years. The American southwest and west continue to become more important politically; however, these are also some of the most diverse regions in the country. Additionally, as the immigrant population increases and more people choose to have children with individuals of other races, the United States is becoming ever more diverse. Additionally, gay, lesbian, and transgender people are increasingly gaining civil rights, as they and their supporters gain political capital as a demographic group. This creates a need for politicians to respond to diversity.

DID YOU KNOW?
This has given rise to a number of human rights abuses in makeshift services (often run by Mexican organized crime groups) that offer passage across the American border.

Immigration has led to high Latin American and Asian American populations in the southwest and west of the United States. While some amount of this immigration occurs through the legal process, many Latin American immigrants enter the country by extralegal means, crossing the border between the United States and Mexico.

In many communities, undocumented immigrants provide a number of services and meet needs otherwise not met within the community. Most take jobs that are unwanted, as they have no alternative. The 1986 Immigration Reform and Control Act addressed some issues of illegal immigration, and allowed some immigrants to gain legal standing; however, both parties agree that broad immigration reform is needed in the United States today.

Another sweeping demographic change is known as "the graying of America." As the average age of the American citizen grows higher and technology and medicine continue to increase the average life span, some economists and politicians have raised questions about the future solvency of some government programs.

The biggest problem facing Social Security is the impending retirement of baby boomers, who will leave the workforce in greater numbers than there are workers paying into the system, thus depleting the assets of the Trust. They will no longer help to keep the system at a ratio of two or more workers per retiree and by the year 2030, twenty-five percent of all Americans drawing on Social Security will be older than eighty-five.

PART II
Resources

CHAPTER TEN
Founding American Documents

In this section, you will find various reference materials and resources that will help you in your studies. Though you will likely not encounter questions on the exam about the specifics of content in historical documents such as the Constitution or the Declaration of Independence, reading and understanding them in full can help provide crucial context to your understanding of U.S. history.

The Declaration of Independence
IN CONGRESS, JULY 4, 1776.

The unanimous Declaration of the thirteen United States of America,

When in the Course of human events it becomes necessary for one people to dissolve the political bands which have connected them with another and to assume among the powers of the earth, the separate and equal station to which the Laws of Nature and of Nature's God entitle them, a decent respect to the opinions of mankind requires that they should declare the causes which impel them to the separation.

We hold these truths to be self-evident, that all men are created equal, that they are endowed by their Creator with certain unalienable Rights, that among these are Life, Liberty and the pursuit of Happiness. — That to secure these rights, Governments are instituted among Men, deriving their just powers from the consent of the governed, — That whenever any Form of Government becomes destructive of these ends, it is the Right of the People to alter or to abolish it, and to institute new Government, laying its foundation on such principles and organizing its powers in such form, as to them shall seem most likely to effect their Safety and Happiness. Prudence, indeed, will dictate that Governments long established should not be changed for light and transient causes; and accordingly all experience hath shewn that mankind are more disposed to suffer, while evils are sufferable than to right themselves by abolishing the forms to which they are accustomed. But when a long train of abuses and usurpations, pursuing invariably the same Object evinces a design to reduce them under absolute Despotism, it is their right, it is their duty, to throw off such Government, and to provide new Guards for their future security. — Such has been the patient sufferance of these Colonies; and such is now the necessity which constrains them to alter their former Systems of Government. The history of the present King of Great Britain is a history of repeated injuries and usurpations, all having in direct object the establishment of an absolute Tyranny over these States. To prove this, let Facts be submitted to a candid world.

He has refused his Assent to Laws, the most wholesome and necessary for the public good.

He has forbidden his Governors to pass Laws of immediate and pressing importance, unless suspended in their operation till his Assent should be obtained; and when so suspended, he has utterly neglected to attend to them.

He has refused to pass other Laws for the accommodation of large districts of people, unless those people would relinquish the right of Representation in the Legislature, a right inestimable to them and formidable to tyrants only.

He has called together legislative bodies at places unusual, uncomfortable, and distant from the depository of their Public Records, for the sole purpose of fatiguing them into compliance with his measures.

He has dissolved Representative Houses repeatedly, for opposing with manly firmness his invasions on the rights of the people.

He has refused for a long time, after such dissolutions, to cause others to be elected, whereby the Legislative Powers, incapable of Annihilation, have returned to the People at large for their exercise; the State remaining in the mean time exposed to all the dangers of invasion from without, and convulsions within.

He has endeavoured to prevent the population of these States; for that purpose obstructing the Laws for Naturalization of Foreigners; refusing to pass others to encourage their migrations hither, and raising the conditions of new Appropriations of Lands.

He has obstructed the Administration of Justice by refusing his Assent to Laws for establishing Judiciary Powers.

He has made Judges dependent on his Will alone for the tenure of their offices, and the amount and payment of their salaries.

He has erected a multitude of New Offices, and sent hither swarms of Officers to harass our people and eat out their substance.

He has kept among us, in times of peace, Standing Armies without the Consent of our legislatures.

He has affected to render the Military independent of and superior to the Civil Power.

He has combined with others to subject us to a jurisdiction foreign to our constitution, and unacknowledged by our laws; giving his Assent to their Acts of pretended Legislation:

For quartering large bodies of armed troops among us:

For protecting them, by a mock Trial from punishment for any Murders which they should commit on the Inhabitants of these States:

For cutting off our Trade with all parts of the world:

For imposing Taxes on us without our Consent:

For depriving us in many cases, of the benefit of Trial by Jury:

For transporting us beyond Seas to be tried for pretended offences:

For abolishing the free System of English Laws in a neighbouring Province, establishing therein an Arbitrary government, and enlarging its Boundaries so as to render it at once an example and fit instrument for introducing the same absolute rule into these Colonies

For taking away our Charters, abolishing our most valuable Laws and altering fundamentally the Forms of our Governments:

For suspending our own Legislatures, and declaring themselves invested with power to legislate for us in all cases whatsoever.

He has abdicated Government here, by declaring us out of his Protection and waging War against us.

He has plundered our seas, ravaged our coasts, burnt our towns, and destroyed the lives of our people.

He is at this time transporting large Armies of foreign Mercenaries to compleat the works of death, desolation, and tyranny, already begun with circumstances of Cruelty & Perfidy scarcely paralleled in the most barbarous ages, and totally unworthy the Head of a civilized nation.

He has constrained our fellow Citizens taken Captive on the high Seas to bear Arms against their Country, to become the executioners of their friends and Brethren, or to fall themselves by their Hands.

He has excited domestic insurrections amongst us, and has endeavoured to bring on the inhabitants of our frontiers, the merciless Indian Savages whose known rule of warfare, is an undistinguished destruction of all ages, sexes and conditions.

In every stage of these Oppressions We have Petitioned for Redress in the most humble terms: Our repeated Petitions have been answered only by repeated injury. A Prince, whose character is thus marked by every act which may define a Tyrant, is unfit to be the ruler of a free people.

Nor have We been wanting in attentions to our British brethren. We have warned them from time to time of attempts by their legislature to extend an unwarrantable jurisdiction over us. We have reminded them of the circumstances of our emigration and settlement here. We have appealed to their native justice and magnanimity, and we have conjured them by the ties of our common kindred to disavow these usurpations, which would inevitably interrupt our connections and correspondence. They too have been deaf to the voice of justice and of consanguinity. We must, therefore, acquiesce in the necessity, which denounces our Separation, and hold them, as we hold the rest of mankind, Enemies in War, in Peace Friends.

We, therefore, the Representatives of the united States of America, in General Congress, Assembled, appealing to the Supreme Judge of the world for the rectitude of our intentions, do, in the Name, and by Authority of the good People of these Colonies, solemnly publish and declare, That these united Colonies are, and of Right ought to be Free and Independent States, that they are Absolved from all Allegiance to the British Crown, and that all political connection between them and the State of Great Britain, is and ought to be totally dissolved; and that as Free and Independent States, they have full Power to levy War, conclude Peace, contract Alliances, establish Commerce, and to do all other Acts and Things which Independent States may of right do. — And for the support of this Declaration, with a firm reliance on the protection of Divine Providence, we mutually pledge to each other our Lives, our Fortunes, and our sacred Honor.

NEW HAMPSHIRE

Josiah Bartlett, William Whipple, Matthew Thornton

MASSACHUSETTS

John Hancock, Samuel Adams, John Adams, Robert Treat Paine, Elbridge Gerry

RHODE ISLAND

Stephen Hopkins, William Ellery

CONNECTICUT

Roger Sherman, Samuel Huntington, William Williams, Oliver Wolcott

NEW YORK

William Floyd, Philip Livingston, Francis Lewis, Lewis Morris

NEW JERSEY

Richard Stockton, John Witherspoon, Francis Hopkinson, John Hart, Abraham Clark

PENNSYLVANIA

Robert Morris, Benjamin Rush, Benjamin Franklin, John Morton, George Clymer, James Smith, George Taylor, James Wilson, George Ross

DELAWARE

Caesar Rodney, George Read, Thomas McKean

MARYLAND

Samuel Chase, William Paca, Thomas Stone, Charles Carroll of Carrollton

VIRGINIA

George Wythe, Richard Henry Lee, Thomas Jefferson, Benjamin Harrison, Thomas Nelson, Jr., Francis Lightfoot Lee, Carter Braxton

NORTH CAROLINA

William Hooper, Joseph Hewes, John Penn

SOUTH CAROLINA

Edward Rutledge, Thomas Heyward, Jr., Thomas Lynch, Jr., Arthur Middleton

GEORGIA

Button Gwinnett, Lyman Hall, George Walton

The Constitution
PREAMBLE

We the People of the United States, in Order to form a more perfect Union, establish Justice, insure domestic Tranquility, provide for the common defence, promote the general Welfare, and secure the Blessings of Liberty to ourselves and our Posterity, do ordain and establish this Constitution for the United States of America.

ARTICLE ONE

SECTION. 1. All legislative Powers herein granted shall be vested in a Congress of the United States, which shall consist of a Senate and House of Representatives.

SECTION. 2. The House of Representatives shall be composed of Members chosen every second Year by the People of the several States, and the Electors in each State shall have the Qualifications requisite for Electors of the most numerous Branch of the State Legislature.

No Person shall be a Representative who shall not have attained to the Age of twenty five Years, and been seven Years a Citizen of the United States, and who shall not, when elected, be an Inhabitant of that State in which he shall be chosen.

Representatives and direct Taxes shall be apportioned among the several States which may be included within this Union, according to their respective Numbers, which shall be determined by adding to the whole Number of free Persons, including those bound to Service for a Term of Years, and excluding Indians not taxed, three fifths of all other Persons. The actual Enumeration shall be made within three Years after the first Meeting of the Congress of the United States, and within every subsequent Term of ten Years, in such Manner as they shall by Law direct.The number of Representatives shall not exceed one for every thirty Thousand, but each State shall have at Least one Representative; and until such enumeration shall be made, the State of New Hampshire shall be entitled to chuse three, Massachusetts eight, Rhode-Island and Providence Plantations one, Connecticut five, New-York six, New Jersey four, Pennsylvania eight, Delaware one, Maryland six, Virginia ten, North Carolina five, South Carolina five, and Georgia three.

When vacancies happen in the Representation from any State, the Executive Authority thereof shall issue Writs of Election to fill such Vacancies.

The House of Representatives shall chuse their Speaker and other Officers;and shall have the sole Power of Impeachment.

SECTION. 3. The Senate of the United States shall be composed of two Senators from each State, chosen by the Legislature thereof, for six Years; and each Senator shall have one Vote.

Immediately after they shall be assembled in Consequence of the first Election, they shall be divided as equally as may be into three Classes. The Seats of the Senators of the first Class shall be vacated at the Expiration of the second Year, of the second Class at the Expiration of the fourth Year, and of the third Class at the Expiration of the sixth Year, so that one third may be chosen every second Year;and if Vacancies happen by Resignation, or otherwise, during the Recess of the Legislature of any State, the Executive thereof may make temporary Appointments until the next Meeting of the Legislature, which shall then fill such Vacancies.

No Person shall be a Senator who shall not have attained to the Age of thirty Years, and been nine Years a Citizen of the United States, and who shall not, when elected, be an Inhabitant of that State for which he shall be chosen.

The Vice President of the United States shall be President of the Senate, but shall have no Vote, unless they be equally divided.

The Senate shall chuse their other Officers, and also a President pro tempore, in the Absence of the Vice President, or when he shall exercise the Office of President of the United States.

The Senate shall have the sole Power to try all Impeachments. When sitting for that Purpose, they shall be on Oath or Affirmation. When the President of the United

States is tried, the Chief Justice shall preside: And no Person shall be convicted without the Concurrence of two thirds of the Members present.

Judgment in Cases of Impeachment shall not extend further than to removal from Office, and disqualification to hold and enjoy any Office of honor, Trust or Profit under the United States: but the Party convicted shall nevertheless be liable and subject to Indictment, Trial, Judgment and Punishment, according to Law.

SECTION. 4. The Times, Places and Manner of holding Elections for Senators and Representatives, shall be prescribed in each State by the Legislature thereof; but the Congress may at any time by Law make or alter such Regulations, except as to the Places of chusing Senators.

The Congress shall assemble at least once in every Year, and such Meeting shall be on the first Monday in December, unless they shall by Law appoint a different Day.

SECTION. 5. Each House shall be the Judge of the Elections, Returns and Qualifications of its own Members, and a Majority of each shall constitute a Quorum to do Business; but a smaller Number may adjourn from day to day, and may be authorized to compel the Attendance of absent Members, in such Manner, and under such Penalties as each House may provide.

Each House may determine the Rules of its Proceedings, punish its Members for disorderly Behaviour, and, with the Concurrence of two thirds, expel a Member.

Each House shall keep a Journal of its Proceedings, and from time to time publish the same, excepting such Parts as may in their Judgment require Secrecy; and the Yeas and Nays of the Members of either House on any question shall, at the Desire of one fifth of those Present, be entered on the Journal.

Neither House, during the Session of Congress, shall, without the Consent of the other, adjourn for more than three days, nor to any other Place than that in which the two Houses shall be sitting.

SECTION. 6. The Senators and Representatives shall receive a Compensation for their Services, to be ascertained by Law, and paid out of the Treasury of the United States. They shall in all Cases, except Treason, Felony and Breach of the Peace, be privileged from Arrest during their Attendance at the Session of their respective Houses, and in going to and returning from the same; and for any Speech or Debate in either House, they shall not be questioned in any other Place.

No Senator or Representative shall, during the Time for which he was elected, be appointed to any civil Office under the Authority of the United States, which shall have been created, or the Emoluments whereof shall have been encreased during such time; and no Person holding any Office under the United States, shall be a Member of either House during his Continuance in Office.

SECTION. 7. All Bills for raising Revenue shall originate in the House of Representatives; but the Senate may propose or concur with Amendments as on other Bills.

Every Bill which shall have passed the House of Representatives and the Senate, shall, before it become a Law, be presented to the President of the United States; If he approve he shall sign it, but if not he shall return it, with his Objections to that House in which it shall have originated, who shall enter the Objections at large on their Journal, and proceed to reconsider it. If after such Reconsideration two thirds of that House shall agree to pass the Bill, it shall be sent, together with the Objections, to the other House, by which it shall likewise be reconsidered, and if approved by two thirds of that House, it shall become a Law. But in all such Cases the Votes of both Houses shall be determined by Yeas and Nays, and the Names of the Persons voting for and against the Bill shall be entered on the Journal of each House respectively. If any Bill shall not be returned by the President within ten Days (Sundays excepted) after it shall have been presented to him, the Same shall be a Law, in like Manner as if he had signed it, unless the Congress by their Adjournment prevent its Return, in which Case it shall not be a Law.

Every Order, Resolution, or Vote to which the Concurrence of the Senate and House of Representatives may be necessary (except on a question of Adjournment) shall be presented to the President of the United States; and before the Same shall take Effect, shall be approved by him, or being disapproved by him, shall be repassed by two thirds of the Senate and House of Representatives, according to the Rules and Limitations prescribed in the Case of a Bill.

SECTION. 8. The Congress shall have Power To lay and collect Taxes, Duties, Imposts and Excises, to pay the Debts and provide for the common Defence and general Welfare of the United States; but all Duties, Imposts and Excises shall be uniform throughout the United States;

To borrow Money on the credit of the United States;

To regulate Commerce with foreign Nations, and among the several States, and with the Indian Tribes;

To establish an uniform Rule of Naturalization, and uniform Laws on the subject of Bankruptcies throughout the United States;

To coin Money, regulate the Value thereof, and of foreign Coin, and fix the Standard of Weights and Measures;

To provide for the Punishment of counterfeiting the Securities and current Coin of the United States;

To establish Post Offices and post Roads;

To promote the Progress of Science and useful Arts, by securing for limited Times to Authors and Inventors the exclusive Right to their respective Writings and Discoveries;

To constitute Tribunals inferior to the supreme Court;

To define and punish Piracies and Felonies committed on the high Seas, and Offenses against the Law of Nations;

To declare War, grant Letters of Marque and Reprisal, and make Rules concerning Captures on Land and Water;

To raise and support Armies, but no Appropriation of Money to that Use shall be for a longer Term than two Years;

To provide and maintain a Navy; To make Rules for the Government and Regulation of the land and naval Forces;

To provide for calling forth the Militia to execute the Laws of the Union, suppress Insurrections and repel Invasions;

To provide for organizing, arming, and disciplining, the Militia, and for governing such Part of them as may be employed in the Service of the United States, reserving to the States respectively, the Appointment of the Officers, and the Authority of training the Militia according to the discipline prescribed by Congress;

To exercise exclusive Legislation in all Cases whatsoever, over such District (not exceeding ten Miles square) as may, by Cession of particular States, and the Acceptance of Congress, become the Seat of the Government of the United States, and to exercise like Authority over all Places purchased by the Consent of the Legislature of the State in which the Same shall be, for the Erection of Forts, Magazines, Arsenals, dock-Yards and other needful Buildings;-And

To make all Laws which shall be necessary and proper for carrying into Execution the foregoing Powers, and all other Powers vested by this Constitution in the Government of the United States, or in any Department or Officer thereof.

SECTION. 9. The Migration or Importation of such Persons as any of the States now existing shall think proper to admit, shall not be prohibited by the Congress prior to the Year one thousand eight hundred and eight, but a Tax or duty may be imposed on such Importation, not exceeding ten dollars for each Person.

The Privilege of the Writ of Habeas Corpus shall not be suspended, unless when in Cases of Rebellion or Invasion the public Safety may require it.

No Bill of Attainder or ex post facto Law shall be passed.

No Capitation, or other direct, Tax shall be laid, unless in Proportion to the Census or Enumeration herein before directed to be taken.

No Tax or Duty shall be laid on Articles exported from any State.

No Preference shall be given by any Regulation of Commerce or Revenue to the Ports of one State over those of another: nor shall Vessels bound to, or from, one State, be obliged to enter, clear, or pay Duties in another.

No Money shall be drawn from the Treasury, but in Consequence of Appropriations made by Law; and a regular Statement and Account of the Receipts and Expenditures of all public Money shall be published from time to time.

No Title of Nobility shall be granted by the United States: And no Person holding any Office of Profit or Trust under them, shall, without the Consent of the Congress, accept of any present, Emolument, Office, or Title, of any kind whatever, from any King, Prince, or foreign State.

SECTION. 10. No State shall enter into any Treaty, Alliance, or Confederation; grant Letters of Marque and Reprisal; coin Money; emit Bills of Credit; make any Thing but gold and silver Coin a Tender in Payment of Debts; pass any Bill of Attainder, ex post facto Law, or Law impairing the Obligation of Contracts, or grant any Title of Nobility.

No State shall, without the Consent of the Congress, lay any Imposts or Duties on Imports or Exports, except what may be absolutely necessary for executing it's inspection Laws: and the net Produce of all Duties and Imposts, laid by any State on Imports or Exports, shall be for the Use of the Treasury of the United States; and all such Laws shall be subject to the Revision and Controul of the Congress.

No State shall, without the Consent of Congress, lay any Duty of Tonnage, keep Troops, or Ships of War in time of Peace, enter into any Agreement or Compact with another State, or with a foreign Power, or engage in War, unless actually invaded, or in such imminent Danger as will not admit of delay.

ARTICLE II

SECTION. 1. The executive Power shall be vested in a President of the United States of America. He shall hold his Office during the Term of four Years, and, together with the Vice President, chosen for the same Term, be elected, as follows:

Each State shall appoint, in such Manner as the Legislature thereof may direct, a Number of Electors, equal to the whole Number of Senators and Representatives to which the State may be entitled in the Congress: but no Senator or Representative, or Person holding an Office of Trust or Profit under the United States, shall be appointed an Elector.

The Electors shall meet in their respective States, and vote by Ballot for two Persons, of whom one at least shall not be an Inhabitant of the same State with themselves. And they shall make a List of all the Persons voted for, and of the Number of Votes for each; which List they shall sign and certify, and transmit sealed to the Seat of the Government of the United States, directed to the President of the Senate. The President of the Senate shall, in the Presence of the Senate and House of Representatives, open all the Certificates, and the Votes shall then be counted. The Person having the greatest Number of Votes shall be the President, if such Number be a Majority of the whole

Number of Electors appointed; and if there be more than one who have such Majority, and have an equal Number of Votes, then the House of Representatives shall immediately chuse by Ballot one of them for President; and if no Person have a Majority, then from the five highest on the List the said House shall in like Manner chuse the President. But in chusing the President, the Votes shall be taken by States, the Representation from each State having one Vote; A quorum for this Purpose shall consist of a Member or Members from two thirds of the States, and a Majority of all the States shall be necessary to a Choice. In every Case, after the Choice of the President, the Person having the greatest Number of Votes of the Electors shall be the Vice President. But if there should remain two or more who have equal Votes, the Senate shall chuse from them by Ballot the Vice President.

The Congress may determine the Time of chusing the Electors, and the Day on which they shall give their Votes; which Day shall be the same throughout the United States.

No Person except a natural born Citizen, or a Citizen of the United States, at the time of the Adoption of this Constitution, shall be eligible to the Office of President; neither shall any person be eligible to that Office who shall not have attained to the Age of thirty five Years, and been fourteen Years a Resident within the United States.

In Case of the Removal of the President from Office, or of his Death, Resignation, or Inability to discharge the Powers and Duties of the said Office, the Same shall devolve on the Vice President, and the Congress may by Law provide for the Case of Removal, Death, Resignation or Inability, both of the President and Vice President, declaring what Officer shall then act as President, and such Officer shall act accordingly, until the Disability be removed, or a President shall be elected.

The President shall, at stated Times, receive for his Services, a Compensation, which shall neither be increased nor diminished during the Period for which he shall have been elected, and he shall not receive within that Period any other Emolument from the United States, or any of them.

Before he enter on the Execution of his Office, he shall take the following Oath or Affirmation:--"I do solemnly swear (or affirm) that I will faithfully execute the Office of President of the United States, and will to the best of my Ability, preserve, protect and defend the Constitution of the United States."

SECTION. 2. The President shall be Commander in Chief of the Army and Navy of the United States, and of the Militia of the several States, when called into the actual Service of the United States; he may require the Opinion, in writing, of the principal Officer in each of the executive Departments, upon any Subject relating to the Duties of their respective Offices, and he shall have Power to grant Reprieves and Pardons for Offenses against the United States, except in Cases of Impeachment.

He shall have Power, by and with the Advice and Consent of the Senate, to make Treaties, provided two thirds of the Senators present concur; and he shall nominate, and by and with the Advice and Consent of the Senate, shall appoint Ambassadors, other public Ministers and Consuls, Judges of the supreme Court, and all other Officers of the United States, whose Appointments are not herein otherwise provided for, and which shall be established by Law: but the Congress may by Law vest the Appointment of such inferior Officers, as they think proper, in the President alone, in the Courts of Law, or in the Heads of Departments.

The President shall have Power to fill up all Vacancies that may happen during the Recess of the Senate, by granting Commissions which shall expire at the End of their next Session.

SECTION. 3. He shall from time to time give to the Congress Information of the State of the Union, and recommend to their Consideration such Measures as he shall judge necessary and expedient; he may, on extraordinary Occasions, convene both Houses, or either of them, and in Case of Disagreement between them, with Respect to the Time of Adjournment, he may adjourn them to such Time as he shall think proper; he shall receive Ambassadors and other public Ministers; he shall take Care that the Laws be faithfully executed, and shall Commission all the Officers of the United States.

SECTION. 4. The President, Vice President and all civil Officers of the United States, shall be removed from Office on Impeachment for, and Conviction of, Treason, Bribery, or other high Crimes and Misdemeanors.

ARTICLE III

SECTION. 1. The judicial Power of the United States, shall be vested in one supreme Court, and in such inferior Courts as the Congress may from time to time ordain and establish. The Judges, both of the supreme and inferior Courts, shall hold their Offices during good Behaviour, and shall, at stated Times, receive for their Services, a Compensation, which shall not be diminished during their Continuance in Office.

SECTION. 2. The judicial Power shall extend to all Cases, in Law and Equity, arising under this Constitution, the Laws of the United States, and Treaties made, or which shall be made, under their Authority;--to all Cases affecting Ambassadors, other public Ministers and Consuls;--to all Cases of admiralty and maritime Jurisdiction;--to Controversies to which the United States shall be a Party;--to Controversies between two or more States;--between a State and Citizens of another State;--between Citizens of different States;--between Citizens of the same State claiming Lands under Grants of different States, and between a State, or the Citizens thereof, and foreign States, Citizens or Subjects.

In all Cases affecting Ambassadors, other public Ministers and Consuls, and those in which a State shall be Party, the supreme Court shall have original Jurisdiction. In all the other Cases before mentioned, the supreme Court shall have appellate Jurisdiction, both as to Law and Fact, with such Exceptions, and under such Regulations as the Congress shall make.

The Trial of all Crimes, except in Cases of Impeachment; shall be by Jury; and such Trial shall be held in the State where the said Crimes shall have been committed; but when not committed within any State, the Trial shall be at such Place or Places as the Congress may by Law have directed.

SECTION. 3. Treason against the United States, shall consist only in levying War against them, or in adhering to their Enemies, giving them Aid and Comfort. No Person shall be convicted of Treason unless on the Testimony of two Witnesses to the same overt Act, or on Confession in open Court.

The Congress shall have Power to declare the Punishment of Treason, but no Attainder of Treason shall work Corruption of Blood, or Forfeiture except during the Life of the Person attainted.

ARTICLE IV

SECTION. 1. Full Faith and Credit shall be given in each State to the public Acts, Records, and judicial Proceedings of every other State. And the Congress may by general Laws prescribe the Manner in which such Acts, Records and Proceedings shall be proved, and the Effect thereof.

SECTION. 2. The Citizens of each State shall be entitled to all Privileges and Immunities of Citizens in the several States.

A Person charged in any State with Treason, Felony, or other Crime, who shall flee from Justice, and be found in another State, shall on Demand of the executive Authority of the State from which he fled, be delivered up, to be removed to the State having Jurisdiction of the Crime.

No Person held to Service or Labour in one State, under the Laws thereof, escaping into another, shall, in Consequence of any Law or Regulation therein, be discharged from such Service or Labour, but shall be delivered up on Claim of the Party to whom such Service or Labour may be due.

SECTION. 3. New States may be admitted by the Congress into this Union; but no new State shall be formed or erected within the Jurisdiction of any other State; nor any State be formed by the Junction of two or more States, or Parts of States, without the Consent of the Legislatures of the States concerned as well as of the Congress.

The Congress shall have Power to dispose of and make all needful Rules and Regulations respecting the Territory or other Property belonging to the United States; and nothing in this Constitution shall be so construed as to Prejudice any Claims of the United States, or of any particular State.

SECTION. 4. The United States shall guarantee to every State in this Union a Republican Form of Government, and shall protect each of them against Invasion; and on Application of the Legislature, or of the Executive (when the Legislature cannot be convened) against domestic Violence.

ARTICLE V

The Congress, whenever two thirds of both Houses shall deem it necessary, shall propose Amendments to this Constitution, or, on the Application of the Legislatures of two thirds of the several States, shall call a Convention for proposing Amendments, which, in either Case, shall be valid to all Intents and Purposes, as Part of this Constitution, when ratified by the Legislatures of three fourths of the several States, or by Conventions in three fourths thereof, as the one or the other Mode of Ratification may be proposed by the Congress; Provided that no Amendment which may be made prior to the Year One thousand eight hundred and eight shall in any Manner affect the first and fourth Clauses in the Ninth Section of the first Article; and that no State, without its Consent, shall be deprived of its equal Suffrage in the Senate.

ARTICLE VI

All Debts contracted and Engagements entered into, before the Adoption of this Constitution, shall be as valid against the United States under this Constitution, as under the Confederation.

This Constitution, and the Laws of the United States which shall be made in Pursuance thereof; and all Treaties made, or which shall be made, under the Authority of the United States, shall be the supreme Law of the Land; and the Judges in every State shall be bound thereby, any Thing in the Constitution or Laws of any State to the Contrary notwithstanding.

The Senators and Representatives before mentioned, and the Members of the several State Legislatures, and all executive and judicial Officers, both of the United States and of the several States, shall be bound by Oath or Affirmation, to support this Constitution; but no religious Test shall ever be required as a Qualification to any Office or public Trust under the United States.

ARTICLE VII

The Ratification of the Conventions of nine States, shall be sufficient for the Establishment of this Constitution between the States so ratifying the Same.

The Bill of Rights

1. Congress shall make no law respecting an establishment of religion, or prohibiting the free exercise thereof; or abridging the freedom of speech, or of the press; or the right of the people peaceably to assemble, and to petition the government for a redress of grievances.

2. A well regulated militia, being necessary to the security of a free state, the right of the people to keep and bear arms, shall not be infringed.

3. No soldier shall, in time of peace be quartered in any house, without the consent of the owner, nor in time of war, but in a manner to be prescribed by law.

4. The right of the people to be secure in their persons, houses, papers, and effects, against unreasonable searches and seizures, shall not be violated, and no warrants shall issue, but upon probable cause, supported by oath or affirmation, and particularly describing the place to be searched, and the persons or things to be seized.

5. No person shall be held to answer for a capital, or otherwise infamous crime, unless on a presentment or indictment of a grand jury, except in cases arising in the land or naval forces, or in the militia, when in actual service in time of war or public danger; nor shall any person be subject for the same offense to be twice put in jeopardy of life or limb; nor shall be compelled in any criminal case to be a witness against himself, nor be deprived of life, liberty, or property, without due process of law; nor shall private property be taken for public use, without just compensation.

6. In all criminal prosecutions, the accused shall enjoy the right to a speedy and public trial, by an impartial jury of the state and district wherein the crime shall have been committed, which district shall have been previously ascertained by law, and to be informed of the nature and cause of the accusation; to be confronted with the witnesses against him; to have compulsory process for obtaining witnesses in his favor, and to have the assistance of counsel for his defense.

7. In suits at common law, where the value in controversy shall exceed twenty dollars, the right of trial by jury shall be preserved, and no fact tried by a jury, shall be otherwise reexamined in any court of the U.S., than according to the rules of the common law.

8. Excessive bail shall not be required, nor excessive fines imposed, nor cruel and unusual punishments inflicted.

9. The enumeration in the Constitution, of certain rights, shall not be construed to deny or disparage others retained by the people.

10. The powers not delegated to the U.S. by the Constitution, nor prohibited by it to the states, are reserved to the states respectively, or to the people.

Amendments 11–27

11. The Judicial power of the United States shall not be construed to extend to any suit in law or equity, commenced or prosecuted against one of the United States by Citizens of another State, or by Citizens or Subjects of any Foreign State.

12. The Electors shall meet in their respective states and vote by ballot for President and Vice-President, one of whom, at least, shall not be an inhabitant of the same state with themselves; they shall name in their ballots the person voted for as President, and in distinct ballots the person voted for as Vice-President, and they shall make distinct lists of all persons voted for as President, and of all persons voted for as Vice-President, and of the number of votes for each, which lists they shall sign and certify, and transmit sealed to the seat of the government of the United States, directed to the President of the Senate; -- The President of the Senate shall, in the presence of the Senate and House of Representatives, open all the certificates and the votes shall then be counted; -- The person having the greatest number of votes for President, shall be the President, if such number be a majority of the whole number of Electors appointed; and if no person have such majority, then from the persons having the highest numbers not exceeding three on the list of those voted for as President, the House of Representatives shall choose immediately, by ballot, the President. But in choosing the President, the votes shall be taken by states, the representation from each state having one vote; a quorum for this purpose shall consist of a member or members from two-thirds of the states, and a majority of all the states shall be necessary to a choice. And if the House of Representatives shall not choose a President whenever the right of choice shall devolve upon them, before the fourth day of March next following, then the Vice-President shall act as President, as in case of the death or other constitutional disability of the President.-- The person having the greatest number of votes as Vice-President, shall be the Vice-President, if such number be a majority of the whole number of Electors appointed, and if no person have a majority, then from the two highest numbers on the list, the Senate shall choose the Vice-President; a quorum for the purpose shall consist of two-thirds of the whole number of Senators, and a majority of the whole number shall be necessary to a

choice. But no person constitutionally ineligible to the office of President shall be eligible to that of Vice-President of the United States.

13. SECTION. 1. Neither slavery nor involuntary servitude, except as a punishment for crime whereof the party shall have been duly convicted, shall exist within the United States, or any place subject to their jurisdiction.

SECTION. 2. Congress shall have power to enforce this article by appropriate legislation.

14. SECTION. 1. All persons born or naturalized in the United States, and subject to the jurisdiction thereof, are citizens of the United States and of the State wherein they reside. No State shall make or enforce any law which shall abridge the privileges or immunities of citizens of the United States; nor shall any State deprive any person of life, liberty, or property, without due process of law; nor deny to any person within its jurisdiction the equal protection of the laws.

SECTION. 2. Representatives shall be apportioned among the several States according to their respective numbers, counting the whole number of persons in each State, excluding Indians not taxed. But when the right to vote at any election for the choice of electors for President and Vice-President of the United States, Representatives in Congress, the Executive and Judicial officers of a State, or the members of the Legislature thereof, is denied to any of the male inhabitants of such State, being twenty-one years of age, and citizens of the United States, or in any way abridged, except for participation in rebellion, or other crime, the basis of representation therein shall be reduced in the proportion which the number of such male citizens shall bear to the whole number of male citizens twenty-one years of age in such State.

SECTION. 3. No person shall be a Senator or Representative in Congress, or elector of President and Vice-President, or hold any office, civil or military, under the United States, or under any State, who, having previously taken an oath, as a member of Congress, or as an officer of the United States, or as a member of any State legislature, or as an executive or judicial officer of any State, to support the Constitution of the United States, shall have engaged in insurrection or rebellion against the same, or given aid or comfort to the enemies thereof. But Congress may by a vote of two-thirds of each House, remove such disability.

SECTION. 4. The validity of the public debt of the United States, authorized by law, including debts incurred for payment of pensions and bounties for services in suppressing insurrection or rebellion, shall not be questioned. But neither the United States nor any State shall assume or pay any debt or obligation incurred in aid of insurrection or rebellion against the United States, or any claim for the loss or emancipation of any slave; but all such debts, obligations and claims shall be held illegal and void.

SECTION. 5. The Congress shall have the power to enforce, by appropriate legislation, the provisions of this article.

15. SECTION. 1. The right of citizens of the United States to vote shall not be denied or abridged by the United States or by any State on account of race, color, or previous condition of servitude.

    SECTION. 2. The Congress shall have the power to enforce this article by appropriate legislation.

16. The Congress shall have power to lay and collect taxes on incomes, from whatever source derived, without apportionment among the several States, and without regard to any census or enumeration.

17. The Senate of the United States shall be composed of two Senators from each State, elected by the people thereof, for six years; and each Senator shall have one vote. The electors in each State shall have the qualifications requisite for electors of the most numerous branch of the State legislatures.

    When vacancies happen in the representation of any State in the Senate, the executive authority of such State shall issue writs of election to fill such vacancies: Provided, That the legislature of any State may empower the executive thereof to make temporary appointments until the people fill the vacancies by election as the legislature may direct.

    This amendment shall not be so construed as to affect the election or term of any Senator chosen before it becomes valid as part of the Constitution.

18. SECTION. 1. After one year from the ratification of this article the manufacture, sale, or transportation of intoxicating liquors within, the importation thereof into, or the exportation thereof from the United States and all territory subject to the jurisdiction thereof for beverage purposes is hereby prohibited.

    SECTION. 2. The Congress and the several States shall have concurrent power to enforce this article by appropriate legislation.

    SECTION. 3. This article shall be inoperative unless it shall have been ratified as an amendment to the Constitution by the legislatures of the several States, as provided in the Constitution, within seven years from the date of the submission hereof to the States by the Congress.

19. The right of citizens of the United States to vote shall not be denied or abridged by the United States or by any State on account of sex.

    Congress shall have power to enforce this article by appropriate legislation.

20. SECTION. 1. The terms of the President and the Vice President shall end at noon on the 20th day of January, and the terms of Senators and Representatives at noon on the 3d day of January, of the years in which such terms would have ended if this article had not been ratified; and the terms of their successors shall then begin.

SECTION. 2. The Congress shall assemble at least once in every year, and such meeting shall begin at noon on the 3d day of January, unless they shall by law appoint a different day.

SECTION. 3. If, at the time fixed for the beginning of the term of the President, the President elect shall have died, the Vice President elect shall become President. If a President shall not have been chosen before the time fixed for the beginning of his term, or if the President elect shall have failed to qualify, then the Vice President elect shall act as President until a President shall have qualified; and the Congress may by law provide for the case wherein neither a President elect nor a Vice President shall have qualified, declaring who shall then act as President, or the manner in which one who is to act shall be selected, and such person shall act accordingly until a President or Vice President shall have qualified.

SECTION. 4. The Congress may by law provide for the case of the death of any of the persons from whom the House of Representatives may choose a President whenever the right of choice shall have devolved upon them, and for the case of the death of any of the persons from whom the Senate may choose a Vice President whenever the right of choice shall have devolved upon them.

SECTION. 5. Sections 1 and 2 shall take effect on the 15th day of October following the ratification of this article.

SECTION. 6. This article shall be inoperative unless it shall have been ratified as an amendment to the Constitution by the legislatures of three-fourths of the several States within seven years from the date of its submission.

21. SECTION. 1. The eighteenth article of amendment to the Constitution of the United States is hereby repealed.

SECTION. 2. The transportation or importation into any State, Territory, or Possession of the United States for delivery or use therein of intoxicating liquors, in violation of the laws thereof, is hereby prohibited.

SECTION. 3. This article shall be inoperative unless it shall have been ratified as an amendment to the Constitution by conventions in the several States, as provided in the Constitution, within seven years from the date of the submission hereof to the States by the Congress.

22. SECTION. 1. No person shall be elected to the office of the President more than twice, and no person who has held the office of President, or acted as President, for more than two years of a term to which some other person was elected President shall be elected to the office of President more than once. But this Article shall not apply to any person holding the office of President when this Article was proposed by Congress, and shall not prevent any person who may be holding the office of President, or acting as President, during the term within which this Article becomes operative from holding the office of President or acting as President during the remainder of such term.

SECTION. 2. This article shall be inoperative unless it shall have been ratified as an amendment to the Constitution by the legislatures of three-fourths of the several States within seven years from the date of its submission to the States by the Congress.

23. SECTION. 1. The District constituting the seat of Government of the United States shall appoint in such manner as Congress may direct:
A number of electors of President and Vice President equal to the whole number of Senators and Representatives in Congress to which the District would be entitled if it were a State, but in no event more than the least populous State; they shall be in addition to those appointed by the States, but they shall be considered, for the purposes of the election of President and Vice President, to be electors appointed by a State; and they shall meet in the District and perform such duties as provided by the twelfth article of amendment.

SECTION. 2. The Congress shall have power to enforce this article by appropriate legislation.

24. SECTION. 1. The right of citizens of the United States to vote in any primary or other election for President or Vice President, for electors for President or Vice President, or for Senator or Representative in Congress, shall not be denied or abridged by the United States or any State by reason of failure to pay poll tax or other tax.

SECTION. 2. The Congress shall have power to enforce this article by appropriate legislation.

25. SECTION. 1. In case of the removal of the President from office or of his death or resignation, the Vice President shall become President.

SECTION. 2. Whenever there is a vacancy in the office of the Vice President, the President shall nominate a Vice President who shall take office upon confirmation by a majority vote of both Houses of Congress.

SECTION. 3. Whenever the President transmits to the President pro tempore of the Senate and the Speaker of the House of Representatives his written declaration that he is unable to discharge the powers and duties of his office, and until he transmits to them a written declaration to the contrary, such powers and duties shall be discharged by the Vice President as Acting President.

SECTION. 4. Whenever the Vice President and a majority of either the principal officers of the executive departments or of such other body as Congress may by law provide, transmit to the President pro tempore of the Senate and the Speaker of the House of Representatives their written declaration that the President is unable to discharge the powers and duties of his office, the Vice President shall immediately assume the powers and duties of the office as Acting President.

Thereafter, when the President transmits to the President pro tempore of the Senate and the Speaker of the House of Representatives his written declaration that no inability exists, he shall resume the powers and duties of his office unless the Vice President and a majority of either the principal officers of the executive department or of such other body as Congress may by law provide, transmit within four days to the President pro tempore of the Senate and the Speaker of the House of Representatives their written declaration that the President is unable to discharge the powers and duties of his office. Thereupon Congress shall decide the issue, assembling within forty-eight hours for that purpose if not in session. If the Congress, within twenty-one days after receipt of the latter written declaration, or, if Congress is not in session, within twenty-one days after Congress is required to assemble, determines by two-thirds vote of both Houses that the President is unable to discharge the powers and duties of his office, the Vice President shall continue to discharge the same as Acting President; otherwise, the President shall resume the powers and duties of his office.

26. SECTION. 1. The right of citizens of the United States, who are eighteen years of age or older, to vote shall not be denied or abridged by the United States or by any State on account of age.

    SECTION. 2. The Congress shall have power to enforce this article by appropriate legislation.

27. No law, varying the compensation for the services of the Senators and Representatives, shall take effect, until an election of representatives shall have intervened.

CHAPTER ELEVEN
Sample Essays

In this section, you will find two sample essay questions that resemble those you might find on the APUSH test. After each, you will read three sample essays: A low quality, average quality, and high quality response. Analyze each essay sample carefully to find the differences between them, and what determines their level of quality. Take notes on your analysis, and study your notes alongside this guide as you prepare to take the exam.

Document-Based Question

Use the following primary source documents to craft an analysis of life on the home front during World War II.

DOCUMENT ONE

"There is one front and one battle where everyone in the U.S.—every man, woman, and child—is in action, and will be privileged to remain in action throughout this war. That front is right here at home, in our daily lives, and in our daily tasks."

– President Franklin D. Roosevelt, 28 April 1942

DOCUMENT TWO

"I think a lot of women said, Screw that noise. 'Cause they had a taste of freedom, they had a taste of making their own money, a taste of spending their own money, making their own decisions. I think the beginning of the women's movement had its seeds right there in World War Two."

– Dellie Hahne, a Red Cross nurse's aide

DOCUMENT THREE

...r gave a lot of people jobs. It led them to expect more than they had ...e. People's expectations, financially, spiritually, were raised. There was ...n a beautiful dream. We were gonna reach the end of the rainbow... I ...member a woman saying on the bus that she hoped the war didn't end until ...she got her refrigerator paid for. An old man hit her over the head with an umbrella. He said, 'How dare you!"

– Peggy Terry, a munitions factory worker

DOCUMENT FOUR

DOCUMENT FIVE

United in this determination and with unshakable faith in the cause for which we fight, we will, with God's help, go forward to our greatest victory.

– General Dwight D. Eisenhower (1944)

LOW-SCORING ESSAY

Americans supported the efforts of the troops in World War II after the attack on Pearl Harbor. Most young men were drafted to serve in the war, and women took the jobs they'd left behind, as well as new ones created by the war. At home, Americans worked to support the troops overseas in a lot of different ways, as called upon by their president, Roosevelt, and later by General Eisenhower, whose message to the troops spoke to the spirt of Americans in the war.

Women went to work, both at home and in factories. They planted gardens, scrimped, saved and canned to make rationing work, encouraged by pamphlets and posters from the government. Many different items were rationed, from fat and sugar to fuel oil and shoes. People were encouraged to make do with what they had, remake things if needed and find new materials not needed for the war effort. Sacrifices at home were made willingly, to support the fighting troops overseas. These measures, as well as production at work, gave those on the home front the ability to contribute.

For some families, the war brought a new level of success and new access to consumer goods, like the refrigerator mentioned above. Some women had a hard time moving from freedom back to married life when the war ended, but most married and settled into the life of the 1950s.

While the transition back to normal life in peace-time was not an easy one, it was a joyous one. At V-day, when the war ended, everyone celebrated. The country had sustained significant losses, but was economically sound and strong. Employment was high and finally, after years of war, troops would be on their way home to rejoin their families.

AVERAGE-SCORING ESSAY

During World War II, most men of fighting age went to war, unless they were physically unable. This left the country to be managed by women and older men, those too old to fight. Many men, even beyond youth, volunteered to serve. While conditions in the U.S. were never as difficult as they were in war zones, Americans made sacrifices to support the troops on the front. Those at home feared another attack, after the December 1941 attack on Pearl Harbor.

Early in the war effort, the American government began requisitioning a wide variety of goods and supplies for the troops. These ranged from leather for boots to silk for parachutes, as well as supplies needed for weaponry, planes, ships and heavy machinery. Americans gathered scrap metal and rubber for recycling. Other supplies were rationed, limiting the amount an individual or family could purchase. Ration coupons allowed people to shop for goods that were limited in the market, including shoes, butter, and meat. Throughout America people were encouraged to grow victory gardens in their homes and communities to help supplement the food supply. Posters and radio announcements reminded people that this was their contribution to the war effort, and that their hard work helped to support the troops, as shown in the ration poster.

Even more important than goods was industrial production. With most men at war, women took their place in factories. Families that had once struggled with poverty experienced a great degree of financial freedom, as shown in the quote of the woman worried about paying off her refrigerator before the end of the war. Women made weapons and planes, and child care facilities were created to allow mothers to work; in this way, women gained a new level of social power. This would challenge many women when men returned home from war, as stated in the quote from one of the women who worked during the war.

The support for the war was broad, with everyone doing their part, as stated by Roosevelt. That did not change when the troops came home. V-day or Victory Day was marked by celebrations. An iconic image of the period, the photo of the sailor and nurse embracing illustrates that. There was, even amidst the losses sustained in the Second World War, no place for sadness as everyone at home celebrated a hard-won victory.

HIGH-SCORING ESSAY

Throughout America, the families of soldiers, sailors, airmen, and nurses, as well as those unable to serve, worked in every way they were able for the success of the war effort and the men fighting on the Eastern and Western Fronts. This help was physical, financial, and practical, enabling everyone, from young to old, to do their part, as stated by Roosevelt in one of his Fireside radio addresses.

Rationing was instituted in 1942 to help meet the needs of the military for food, clothing, goods, and supplies. Families were issued ration coupons to buy various items, including fat, sugar and meat, as well as shoes and some types of clothing. Fuel oil and other supplies were also rationed from 1942 through the end of World War II. Rationing was often difficult and the government worked to encourage it with posters and brochures, as well as cookbooks and other press materials. The American public also pitched in by buying war bonds to help pay for the costs of war. War bonds increased the available cash for the war effort and arming the troops.

Women took the jobs men had left behind, as well as new jobs in the military industry. They built planes and bombs, worked on tanks, and some headed overseas to serve as nurses. With near 100 percent employment, the economy was thriving. Many people had more funds to spend than ever before and could now buy larger consumer goods, making payments on household items, like refrigerators. For the first time, women largely controlled the spending, as well as all other aspects of household management.

When the war was finally won, people celebrated in the streets, as commemorated in the famous image of the sailor and nurse kissing in Times Square. Rationing ended, allowing people to enjoy the new economic success that had come with the war.

The end of World War II did not, necessarily, make for a smooth transition from war to peace for some, leading to general dissatisfaction among women who had known great personal freedom and had since lost it. Nonetheless, in the years after the war, veterans came home, took jobs, married and had children in greater numbers than ever before, called the Baby Boom.

Short Answer Question

Read the question, and then write a short answer arguing your stance.

Identify three ways in which Reconstruction impacted legislation following the Civil War.

- ▶ Explain how these changes were implemented
- ▶ Discuss the success or failure of these measures

LOW-SCORING ESSAY

Reconstruction, or the period after the Civil War, involved a number of legislative changes to put the country back together after the end of the war. Slavery was no longer legal, changing the organization of the South in many ways.

The Thirteenth Amendment ended slavery, making Lincoln's Emancipation Proclamation law. It did not provide for any specifics other than slavery, nor did it provide any sort of transitional services for former slaves. While the Thirteenth Amendment ended slavery, the Fourteenth allowed the government to impose laws on the states and specifically identified citizens of the U.S. The Fifteenth granted all citizens the right to vote.

These legislative changes were quickly ratified, amending the Constitution after the end of the Civil War. While the Civil War amendments created a legal basis for rights for former slaves, they were not fairly or evenly enforced. In the South, the Black Codes replaced slavery, limiting the rights of African-Americans. While they were no longer property, they had few civil liberties or rights.

As the 19th century progressed, these laws were not enforced. This allowed conditions to worsen in the South. Eventually, the courts specifically allowed segregation and voting regulations that severely limited African-American access to the polls. Segregation continued until the Civil Rights movement.

AVERAGE-SCORING ESSAY

The Civil War changed the face of America, as well as the laws of America. The Union victory reunited the nation and brought an end to slavery in the southern states. The country was changed and changes to the Constitution soon followed in an attempt to reunite the government and nation. These included amendments to end slavery, define citizenship and allow the federal government additional control over the states, and extend the vote to all male citizens, including former slaves. These changes made the policies at the end of the war federal law.

Following the ratification of the Thirteenth, Fourteenth and Fifteenth Amendments, the nation experienced a short period of racial diversity. Congress included both whites and African-Americans and had a strong interest in creating a more egalitarian nation. The actions of this Congress, including multiple versions of a Civil Rights Act, were designed to integrate public facilities and prevent discrimination. The Freedmen's Bureau was created to help with the transition from slavery to freedom.

This was a short-lived period from immediately after the Civil War until around 1880, soon followed by a period of conservative, racist, southern dominance in the government. While the legislature was Republican-controlled, the executive and judicial were not. Without the support of the executive or judicial, the legislators were unable to achieve any sort of positive change in the South. During the last twenty years of the

19th century, the Supreme Court deemed the Civil Rights Act unconstitutional, made segregation constitutionally acceptable, and allowed voting regulations which limited the access of African-Americans to the polls.

These changes allowed the Jim Crow laws, poll taxes and literacy tests to exist and continue in the South throughout the first half of the 20th century. The Jim Crow laws finally came to an end with the 1964 Civil Rights Act.

HIGH-SCORING ESSAY

The Civil War took an unbelievable toll on the nation, dividing states, families and friends. After the war finally came to a hard-won end for the Union, the legislature was faced with the essential process of creating new laws to support the regulations imposed upon the southern states. These included plans to rebuild the South, but also laws to enforce the northern victory over the south, including a permanent end to slavery.

The Thirteenth Amendment formally ended slavery, making it unconstitutional and banning it from the entirety of the U.S. The next two Reconstruction amendments dealt with the fates of those many former slaves in the South. The Fourteenth defined former slaves as citizens and specifically identified the laws as applying to the states, as well as the federal government. The Fifteenth extended the vote to all citizens, including those who had been slaves.

With the new amendments in place, former slaves could go to the polls and African-Americans could even be elected to serve in Congress. With a biracial Congress, new laws made their way to the congressional floor. Congress also relied upon federal legislation to create an integrated society. A number of different Civil Rights Acts were designed to allow people of all races to use public facilities, like parks, trains and theaters. These laws did not deal with private establishments, but were certainly intended to begin the process of creating an integrated society.

The work of Congress and the northern states after the Civil War continued for a relatively short period of time. While Congress remained dominated by the Republican Party, Lincoln's party, the executive and Supreme Court were not. Southern Democrats gained control, particularly of the judicial branch of the government.

Later, courts declared the Civil Rights Act unconstitutional. Poll taxes and literacy tests were deemed constitutional and the U.S. stopped enforcing the Fifteenth Amendment. The steps forward after the Civil War were followed by leaps backward, leaving a nation still divided by race.

PART III
Test Your Knowledge

CHAPTER TWELVE
Practice Test One

Multiple-Choice Questions

Read the passage and/or question, and then choose the most correct answer.

Questions 1–5 refer to the following passage.

"A house divided against itself cannot stand. I believe this government cannot endure permanently half slave and half free. I do not expect the Union to be dissolved; I do not expect the house to fall; but I do expect that it will cease to be divided. It will become all the one thing or all the other. Either the opponents of slavery will arrest the further spread of it and place it where the public mind shall rest in the belief that it is in course of ultimate extinction, or its advocates will push it forward until it shall become alike lawful in all the states, old as well as new, north as well as south."

– Abraham Lincoln, June 16, 1858

1. Lincoln's speech, given while a candidate for the U.S. Senate, foreshadows the:
   A. American Civil War
   B. Dred Scott decision
   C. Kansas-Nebraska Act
   D. Missouri Compromise
   E. Secession

2. The Confederate capital was:
   A. Richmond, VA then moved to Montgomery, AL
   B. Montgomery, AL then moved to Richmond, VA
   C. always located in Richmond, VA
   D. always located in Montgomery, AL
   E. Washington, D.C.

3. During the Civil War, as a general rule, the:

A. Confederacy was offensive-minded and attacked Washington, D.C.

B. Union was defensive-minded and defended Washington, D.C.

C. Union was offensive-minded and attacked Confederate territories

D. Confederacy was defensive-minded and defended Richmond, VA

E. Union was defensive-minded and defended Montgomery, AL

4. One of the results of the Civil War was:

A. over 1,000,000 soldiers killed

B. the South's economy was destroyed, but the North's grew

C. the rise of the Federalist Party

D. the rise of the Republican Party

E. the growth of the southern economy

5. As a condition of Robert E. Lee's surrender at Appomattox Court House in Virginia, Lincoln demanded that:

A. the South abolish slavery

B. the South agree to adhere to the Emancipation Proclamation

C. the Confederate troops lay down their arms

D. the South accept the Reconstruction Amendments

E. all of the above

Questions 6 – 9 refer to the following passage.

"We hold that the scriptures are most perfect, containing in them all doctrines needful to salvation, whether they concern faith and manners and therefore we acknowledge no such traditions beside the written word which shall be necessary to salvation, so as he which believeth them not cannot be saved."

– William Perkins, 1597

6. The above passage illustrates the importance of the Bible in Puritan thought. Puritans ultimately believed:

A. there should be a separation between church and state

B. no separation should exist between church and state

C. other religions led to salvation as long as they were Christian-based

D. civil laws were based loosely on The New Testament only

E. government officials were not required to be church members

7. Puritans believed the Bible was:

A. the source of both religious and civil authority

B. to be used as a guideline for morality, but not legal policies

C. to be read only by the Elect, not by the masses

D. to be supplemented by reading other holy books such as the Quran

E. only accurate if it was the Gutenberg edition

8. Basing their beliefs on the Bible, Puritans also believed:

    A. women should have equal rights

    B. a patriarchal society was appropriate

    C. a matriarchal society was appropriate

    D. marriage should be avoided

    E. women should preach in the church

9. The following were most important to Puritan life:

    A. God, colony, village, congregation, family

    B. God, colony, village, congregation, individual

    C. God, colony, village, religious tolerance, family

    D. God, colony, village, congregation, equal rights for all

    E. none of the above

Questions 10 – 14 refer to the following quote.

"I pledge you, I pledge myself, to a new deal for the American people."

– Franklin D. Roosevelt, 1932

10. FDR held "fireside chats," which were:

    A. radio addresses the President gave to the American people

    B. radio addresses featuring The Boys Scouts of America

    C. town hall lectures the President gave throughout the country

    D. a series of committee meetings with his cabinet

    E. a series of meetings with the legislature

11. FDR's New Deal was intended to:

    A. help stimulate the U.S. economy during the Great Depression

    B. urge Congress to declare war on Japan and enter WWI

    C. urge Congress to declare war on Japan and enter WWII

    D. create a new political party

    E. create a foothold for Communism in America

12. Three primary goals of the New Deal were:

    A. relief, recovery, and reform

    B. relief, recovery, and recreation

    C. relief, reform, and reconciliation

    D. recovery, redlining, reconstruction

    E. relief, reform, and repair

13. Which of the following was not a program created from the New Deal?

    A. Tennessee Valley Authority

    B. Works Public Administration

    C. Federal Deposit Insurance Corporation

    D. National Recovery Administration

    E. Federal Bureau of Investigations

14. Perhaps the most significant program of the New Deal, which still exists today, is:

    A. Federal Bureau of Investigations

    B. Public Works Administration

    C. Social Security

    D. Civil Works Administration

    E. Central Intelligence Agency

Questions 15 – 19 refer to the following passage.

"I make my money by supplying a public demand. If I break the law, my customers, who number hundreds of the best people in Chicago, are as guilty as I am. Everybody calls me a racketeer. I call myself a businessman."

– Al Capone, 1925

15. The previous quote directly relates to organized crime's rise due to:
    A. Prohibition
    B. the fact that the FBI had not yet been created
    C. illegal firearm sales
    D. the Patriot Act
    E. women's suffrage

16. Which Amendment to the U.S. Constitution established Prohibition?
    A. 21st
    B. 20th
    C. 19th
    D. 18th
    E. 22nd

17. Prohibition was later repealed by which Amendment?
    A. 21st
    B. 20th
    C. 19th
    D. 18th
    E. 23rd

18. How many Amendments to the U.S. Constitution have repealed previous Amendments?
    A. 1
    B. 2
    C. 3
    D. 4
    E. 5

19. Prohibition was the main goal of what social reform movement?
    A. abolitionist
    B. socialist
    C. temperance
    D. women's suffrage
    E. progressive

Questions 20 – 24 refer to the following passage.

"It seems now to be pretty well understood that the real difference of interests lies not between the large and small but between the northern and southern states. The institution of slavery and its consequences form the line of discrimination."

– James Madison, 1787

20. The above quote from Madison is in response to seats in Congress being determined by states' populations. Which chamber's seats are determined by population?
    A. Senate
    B. House of Representatives
    C. Senate, but only in even numbered years
    D. Supreme Court
    E. Presidential cabinet

21. Madison's quote alludes to the population of Southern states, which generally had a substantial slave population, in determining Congressional seats. Ultimately...

   A. the Three-Fifths Compromise was added to the Constitution

   B. the Three-Fifths Compromise was added to the Articles of Confederation

   C. all Native Americans would count as 3/5ths of a person

   D. all people in slave-owning states would count as 3/5ths of a person

   E. slaves would not count for the purposes of determining population

22. The Three-Fifths Compromise was negated by:

   A. the 13th Amendment

   B. the 14th Amendment

   C. the 15th Amendment

   D. the 16th Amendment

   E. the 12th Amendment

23. Some founding fathers who opposed slavery were open to compromise with Southern states during the Constitutional Convention, believing that it:

   A. would eventually run its course and die out as an institution

   B. would continue indefinitely

   C. would have an Amendment abolishing it in the Bill of Rights

   D. should be limited to states that were south of the Mason-Dixon line

   E. was effectively addressed in the Dred Scott decision

24. Congress passed the Act Prohibiting the Importation of Slaves in:

   A. 1776

   B. 1777

   C. 1789

   D. 1803

   E. 1807

Questions 25 – 29 refer to the following passage.

"The great rule of conduct for us in regard to foreign nations is in extending our commercial relations, to have with them as little political connection as possible. So far as we have already formed engagements, let them be fulfilled with perfect good faith. Here let us stop. Europe has a set of primary interests which to us have none; or a very remote relation. Hence she must be engaged in frequent controversies, the causes of which are essentially foreign to our concerns. Hence, therefore, it must be unwise in us to implicate ourselves by artificial ties in the ordinary vicissitudes of her politics, or the ordinary combinations and collisions of her friendships or enmities."

– George Washington, "Farewell Address," 1796

25. This passage warns against U.S. involvement in foreign affairs, a sentiment that is echoed later in:

   A. the Monroe Doctrine

   B. the NATO Charter

   C. the NAFTA Charter

   D. the U.N. Charter

   E. the Fourteen Points Speech

26. In 1796, these two countries were actively engaged in North American empire-building:

    A. Spain and Italy

    B. Britain and Italy

    C. Britain and Spain

    D. Britain and France

    E. Italy and France

27. The United States would remain relatively neutral in its involvement with foreign conflicts. The United States' first major foreign intervention, which did not take place until the end of the nineteenth century, was in the:

    A. Spanish-American War

    B. American Civil War

    C. War of 1812

    D. French and Indian War

    E. World War I

28. In the "Farewell Address," Washington announces his impending retirement and will not accept a third term in office. All U.S. Presidents followed suit, with no President serving more than two terms except:

    A. Theodore Roosevelt

    B. Abraham Lincoln

    C. Franklin Roosevelt

    D. James Madison

    E. George Bush

29. The Presidential term was limited to two terms by:

    A. the 22nd Amendment

    B. the 10th Amendment

    C. the Two-Term Act

    D. the 19th Amendment

    E. the 24th Amendment

Questions 30–33 refer to the following passage.

"In about three hours from the time we went on board, we had thus broken and thrown overboard every tea chest to be found on the ship, while those in the other ships were disposing of the tea in the same way, at the same time. We were surrounded by the British armed ships, but no attempt was made to resist us."

– George Hewes, Eyewitness Account to the Boston Tea Party, 1773

30. The Boston Tea Party resulted in:

    A. Britain passing the Intolerable Acts

    B. Britain repealing the Intolerable Acts

    C. the Boston Massacre

    D. the Stamp Act

    E. the Revolutionary War

31. The Intolerable Acts included all of the following except the:

    A. Alien & Sedition Acts

    B. Boston Port Act

    C. Massachusetts Government Act

    D. Administration of Justice Act

    E. Quartering Act

32. The Boston Tea Party was a:

    A. riot against British troops

    B. dumping of tea into Boston Harbor by a group of colonists disguised as Native Americans

    C. protest of the Tea Act

    D. part of the Alien and Sedition Acts

    E. part of the Quartering Act

33. The Boston Tea Party would prove to be a key event leading to the:

A. Boston Massacre

B. American Revolution

C. Stamp Act

D. Declaration of Independence

E. Articles of Confederation

Questions 34–38 refer to the following passage.

"During the war, the holders of power in all countries found it necessary to bribe the populations into cooperation by unusual concessions. Wage-earners were allowed a living wage, Hindus were told they were men and brothers, women were given the vote, and young people were allowed to enjoy those innocent pleasures of which the old, in the name of morality, always wish to rob them."

– Bertrand Russell, *Skeptical Essays*, 1928

34. The above passage's reference to "the war" is the major conflict that affected most of Europe between 1914 and 1918, which was:

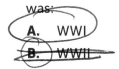

A. WWI

B. WWII

C. Spanish-American War

D. The War of 1812

E. The French and Indian War

35. Women did not receive full suffrage in the United States until 1920 via:

A. the 19th Amendment

B. the Equal Rights Amendment

C. the "Women's Suffrage Act"

D. the Seneca Convention

E. the Civil Rights Act

36. The United States entered the war described in the passage largely because:

A. the Zimmerman Telegram

B. the rise of Nazi Germany

C. the assassination of Franz Ferdinand

D. the attack on the Lusitania

E. the fall of Belgium

37. During the period described in the passage, the U.S. President was:

A. Woodrow Wilson

B. Franklin Roosevelt

C. Theodore Roosevelt

D. Harry Truman

E. Herbert Hoover

38. Within two years after the war, the United States would:

A. join the League of Nations

B. join NATO

C. ratify the Treaty of Versailles

D. join the United Nations

E. none of the above

Questions 39–42 refer to the following passage.

"I know not with what weapons World War III will be fought, but World War IV will be fought with sticks and stones."

– Albert Einstein

39. The United States used atomic weapons to bomb these Japanese cities:

A. Tokyo and Kyoto

B. Tokyo and Hiroshima

C. Hiroshima and Nagasaki

D. Tokyo and Nagasaki

E. Kyoto and Hiroshima

40. In the above passage, Einstein is likely referencing:

- **A.** that atomic weapons have the power to destroy societies and technological progress, setting human beings back to primitive days
- **B.** that atomic weapons used on Japan created widespread death
- **C.** the likelihood that future wars would be less destructive
- **D.** the likelihood that weaponry continues to increase in size and scope
- **E.** that the atomic bomb was the most advanced form of weaponry

41. This event prompted the United States to declare war on Japan and enter WWII:

- **A.** the attack on Pearl Harbor
- **B.** the Zimmerman Telegram
- **C.** the sinking of the Maine
- **D.** the assassination of Franz Ferdinand
- **E.** the sinking of the Lusitania

42. Although Japan and Germany had surrendered earlier, WWII officially ended between the Allies and the countries of Bulgaria, Italy, Finland, and Romania with:

- **A.** the Paris Peace Treaties in 1947
- **B.** the Treaty of Paris in 1920
- **C.** the Treaty of Paris in 1951
- **D.** the Treaty of Paris in 1950
- **E.** none of the above

Questions 43 – 47 refer to the following passage.

"The newspaper is the greatest force in civilization. Under republican government, newspapers form and express public opinion. They suggest and control legislation. They declare wars. They punish criminals, especially the powerful. They reward with approving publicity the good deeds of citizens everywhere. The newspapers control the nation.

– William Randolph Hearst, 1898

43. Hearst was known, along with Joseph Pulitzer, for creating this type of journalism, described as using sensationalism, exaggerations, and poorly researched news stories to sell more newspapers:

- **A.** scandal journalism
- **B.** opinion journalism
- **C.** yellow journalism
- **D.** red journalism
- **E.** tabloid journalism

44. Many point to Hearst and Pulitzer as responsible for the United States' entry into which war?

- **A.** the Civil War
- **B.** the Korean War
- **C.** the Vietnam War
- **D.** the Spanish-American War
- **E.** the War of 1812

45. As a result of the war in question 44, the United States:

- **A.** freed Cuba from Spanish rule
- **B.** drove the North Vietnamese out of South Vietnam
- **C.** defeated the British
- **D.** helped South Korea break away from North Korea
- **E.** was restored as a Union

46. In the war mentioned in question 44, one of the following individuals established himself as a war hero and went on to become President of the United States. Which one?
- **A.** Ulysses S. Grant
- **B.** Andrew Jackson
- **C.** Theodore "Teddy" Roosevelt
- **D.** George Washington
- **E.** Bill Clinton

47. In the war mentioned in question 44, a group of volunteer cavalry soldiers called _____ became famous for acts of valor:
- **A.** Rough Riders
- **B.** The Magnificent Seven
- **C.** 19th Calvary Volunteers
- **D.** Buffalo Soldiers
- **E.** Tuskegee Airmen

Questions 48 – 50 refer to the following passage.

"We don't want a huge flow of illegal immigrants into the United States from Mexico. If you defeat NAFTA, you have to share the responsibility for increased immigration into the United States, where they want jobs that are presently being held by Americans."

– Gerald Ford, 1993

48. NAFTA was signed into law by President:
- **A.** Gerald Ford
- **B.** Ronald Reagan
- **C.** Bill Clinton
- **D.** Barack Obama
- **E.** George W. Bush

49. NAFTA is an acronym for:
- **A.** North American Free Trade Association
- **B.** North American Free Tariff Agreement
- **C.** North American Free Trade Agreement
- **D.** North American Free Tariff Association
- **E.** North American Fair Trade Agreement

50. In the above quote, Ford asserts NAFTA will result in fewer immigrants from Mexico entering the United States illegally. Since NAFTA's inception:
- **A.** there have been fewer immigrants from Mexico who've entered the United States illegally
- **B.** there have been more immigrants from Mexico who've entered the United States illegally
- **C.** the number of immigrants from Mexico has been the same
- **D.** none of the above
- **E.** more immigrants have entered from Mexico legally

Questions 51 – 55 refer to the following quote.

"If there is no struggle, there is no progress."

– Frederick Douglass

51. In the first half of the 19th century, social change driven by religious and social organizations helped to foster political interest in women's rights, abolitionism and utopianism. This was called:

    A.   the Industrial Revolution
    B.   the Second Great Awakening
    C.   the Enlightenment
    D.   the Glorious Revolution
    E.   none of the above

52. This convention on women's rights is often used to mark the beginning of the women's rights movement in the United States:

    A.   the Sioux Falls Convention
    B.   the Constitutional Convention
    C.   the Stonewall Riots
    D.   the Seneca Falls Convention
    E.   the Quaker Society

53. This orator and author published an autobiography that questioned Southern justifications of slavery and argued for abolition:

    A.   Harriet Tubman
    B.   Frederick Douglass
    C.   Martin Luther King, Jr.
    D.   Stephen Douglas
    E.   none of the above

54. This naturalist became famous for his paintings collected in *The Birds of America*:

    A.   Thomas Cole
    B.   Norman Rockwell
    C.   Ansel Adams
    D.   John James Audubon
    E.   Albert Bierstadt

55. The Underground Railroad:

    A.   was a small, elite organization of wealthy Northerners that helped slaves escape to the North
    B.   was an expansive, decentralized network of ordinary people that helped slaves escape to the South
    C.   was an expansive decentralized network of ordinary people that helped slaves escape to the North
    D.   was an expansive, decentralized network of organized criminals that smuggled alcohol across state borders during Prohibition
    E.   was a small, elite organization of women that helped disseminate pro-suffrage literature prior to passage of the 19th Amendment

Short-Answer Questions

Read the passage(s) and question, and then write a short answer arguing your stance.

"But why did the North fight a war rather than simply letting the unhappy Southerners go in peace? It seems unlikely that anyone will ever be able to show that the 'gains' from the war outweighed the 'costs' in economic terms. Still, war is always a gamble, and with neither the costs nor the benefits easily calculated before the fact, leaders are often tempted to take the risk. The evidence above certainly lent strong support for those arguing that it made sense for the South to fight if a belligerent North threatened the institution of slavery. An economic case for the North is more problematic. Most writers argue that the decision for war on Lincoln's part was not based primarily on economic grounds."

– Roger Ransom, *The Economics of the Civil War*

"The cause of the Civil War rests in a form of limbo. A number of alternative explanations awaits evaluation, but there is at present no recognized procedure by which a consensus on the actual cause(s) can be reached."

– Gerald Gunderson, *The Origin of the American Civil War*

1. Based on the above passages, explain the following:

    A. The economic reasons that may have contributed to the American Civil War

    B. Other reasons (social, political, moral) that may have contributed to the American Civil War

---

2. Based on the cartoon above and your knowledge of U.S. history, briefly answer the following questions:

    A. What is the significance of the cartoon as it relates to the United States and the Spanish-American War?

    B. What is "yellow journalism"?

_____
_____
_____
_____
_____
_____
_____
_____
_____
_____
_____
_____
_____
_____
_____
_____
_____
_____
_____
_____
_____
_____
_____

3. Choose one of the following wars and explain how it shaped the United States politically as a world power.

▶ World War I

▶ World War II

----

4. Take your answer from question 3, and compare it to one of the following wars/conflicts to explain how the United States defined itself as a world power:

▶ Vietnam War

▶ Korean War

Document-Based Question

Write an essay using a clearly stated thesis that addresses the question. Use relevant details to support your thesis derived from your knowledge of U.S. history outside the scope of the documents presented. Your answer should position the argument in a broader, historical context.

Analyze the major tenets of Puritan life as it related to their perspectives on religion, family, community, and law.

DOCUMENT ONE

"The fact is, there were all kinds of Puritans. There were dismal precisians, like William Prynne, illiberal and vulgar fanatics, the Tribulation Wholesomes, Hope-on-high Bombys, and Zeal-of-the-land Busys, whose absurdities were the stock in trade of contemporary satirists from Johnson to Butler. But there were also gentlemen and scholars, like Fairfax, Marvell, Colonel Hutchinson, Vane, whose Puritanism was consistent with all elegant tastes and accomplishments. Was Milton's Puritanism hurtful to his art? No and yes. It was in many ways an inspiration; it gave him zeal, a Puritan word much ridiculed by the Royalists; it gave refinement, distinction, selectness, elevation to his picture of the world. But it would be uncritical to deny that it also gave a certain narrowness and rigidity to his view of human life."

– Henry A. Beers, 1920

DOCUMENT TWO

"We must delight in each other, make other's conditions our own, rejoice together, mourn together, labor and suffer together, always having before our eyes our commission and community in the work, our community as members of the same body."

– John Winthrop, 1630

DOCUMENT THREE

"You have spoken diverse things as we have been informed very prejudicial to the honour of the churches and ministers thereof, and you have maintained a meeting and an assembly in your house that hath been condemned by the general assembly as a thing not tolerable nor comely in the sight of God nor fitting for your sex."

– John Winthrop, at the trial of Anne Hutchinson, 1637

DOCUMENT FOUR

"I have been guided by the standard John Winthrop set before his shipmates on the flagship Arbella three hundred and thirty-one years ago, as they, too, faced the task of building a new government on a perilous frontier. 'We must always consider,' he said, 'that we shall be as a city upon a hill – the eyes of all people are upon us.' Today the eyes of all people are truly upon us – and our governments, in every branch, at every level, national, state and local, must be as a city upon a hill – constructed and inhabited by men aware of their great trust and their great responsibilities. For we are setting out upon a voyage in 1961 no less hazardous than that undertaken by the Arbella in 1630."

– John F. Kennedy, 1961

DOCUMENT FIVE

"I never think of the measures necessary for the peace and good order of the colonies without pain. There must be an abridgment of what are called English liberties. I relieve myself by considering that in a remove from a state of nature to the most perfect state of government, there must be a great restraint of natural liberty. I doubt whether it is possible to project a system of government in which a colony 3000 miles distant from the parent state shall enjoy all the liberty of the parent state. I am certain I have never yet seen the projection. I wish the good of the colony when I wish to see some further restraint of liberty rather than the connexion with the parent state should be broken; for I am sure such a breach must prove the ruin of the colony."

– Thomas Hutchinson, 1769

DOCUMENT SIX

"The light of nature showeth that there is a God, who hath lordship and sovereignty over all, is good, and doth good unto all, and is therefore to be feared, loved, praised, called upon, trusted in, and served, with all the heart, and with all the soul, and with all the might. But the acceptable way of worshiping the true God is instituted by himself, and so limited by his own revealed will, that he may not be worshiped according to the imaginations and devices of men, or the suggestions of Satan, under any visible representation, or any other way not prescribed in the Holy Scripture."

– From the "Westminster Confession of Faith," 1646

Long-Essay Question

Write an essay response to the question, using a clear thesis supported by relevant details.

Some historians assert the United States lost the Vietnam War. Based on your knowledge of this conflict and using specific evidence, explain how you agree or disagree with whether the United States lost the Vietnam War.

_____
_____
_____
_____
_____
_____
_____
_____
_____
_____
_____
_____
_____
_____
_____
_____
_____
_____
_____
_____
_____
_____
_____
_____
_____
_____
_____
_____
_____
_____
_____
_____
_____
_____
_____
_____
_____
_____
_____

Answer Key
MULTIPLE-CHOICE

1.	A	29.	A
2.	B	30.	A
3.	C	31.	A
4.	B	32.	E
5.	C	33.	B
6.	B	34.	A
7.	A	35.	A
8.	B	36.	A
9.	A	37.	A
10.	A	38.	E
11.	A	39.	C
12.	A	40.	A
13.	E	41.	A
14.	C	42.	A
15.	A	43.	C
16.	D	44.	D
17.	A	45.	A
18.	A	46.	C
19.	C	47.	A
20.	B	48.	C
21.	D	49.	C
22.	A	50.	B
23.	A	51.	B
24.	E	52.	D
25.	A	53.	B
26.	C	54.	C
27.	A	55.	C
28.	C		

SAMPLE SHORT ANSWERS

1. A number of factors led to the U.S. Civil War. These included moral factors, like slavery, political factors, like secession, and economic factors. The primary economic factor in the war was the difference between North and South. The North was highly industrialized, relying upon raw materials produced in the

South. The South lacked industry or modernization, relied upon slaves, and set itself apart through the secession. These factors contributed not only to the beginning of the war, but also to the eventual Union victory.

2. The Spanish-American War was the result of a number of factors. However, the press played a substantial role in creating public and eventual political support for the war. The key to creating this support was the combined effort of two men, the most prominent newspaper owners and journalists of their time; Pulitzer and Hearst. While these two names are familiar even today, at the time, they were both yellow journalists, producing tabloid style journalism.

3. World War II changed the position of the United States in the world. While world powers were somewhat more balanced, spread throughout the globe, before World War II, there were only two great powers remaining at the end of the war. For many countries, the United States had been a savior, while others, ravaged by war, needed the aid of their former enemy. The United States still had one enemy, communism and the Soviet Union.

4. While World War I had been a great victory, with the support of the population, the Vietnam War was very much the opposite. The conflict in Vietnam lasted some 20 years from its beginnings in the post-war world. U.S. involvement increased progressively over time, until, faced with strong public objects, the United States gradually withdrew, leaving the conflict to the Vietnamese. Communist forces won this war in 1975, after the United States had left.

SAMPLE DOCUMENT-BASED ANSWER

The Puritans were the first Europeans to settle the region now identified as New England. Following the English Civil War, the Puritans sought to leave England and begin a new life, settling down to create communities and organized agricultural villages. While the Puritans left England for political reasons, their society was a staunchly religious one. The Puritans were staunch Protestants with strong objections to the Church of England. Their religious practice was centered on the community church and the community had strict regulations about behavior and conduct.

Puritan communities were relatively small, with each family typically farming a small plot of land. Others had jobs in the community, as servants, smiths, or shopkeepers. Economic success was, for the Puritans, connected closely with religious virtue. The Puritans were Calvinists, who believed that salvation was determined prior to birth; however, success was seen as a means of revealing that salvation. These communities strictly judged anyone who did not conform to norms of social behavior. Adultery, theft, and dishonesty were condemned, but you could also be punished for failing to attend church, swearing, or violating anyone of many minor rules and regulations.

The society of the Puritans began with the family, headed by a patriarchal and powerful husband and father. The wife and mother was submissive, with her children and home her primary care. She was to raise them to be good and godly Puritans. Together, the couple was submissive to God, represented not only by the Divine, but also by their church and community. Puritan communities valued hard work, but had little tolerance for leisure. Reading was acceptable, but religious texts were the only appropriate choice. Dancing was not at all acceptable, nor was gambling.

Many Puritans believed in the existence of demons and other evil supernatural forces. The community of Salem, Massachusetts was Puritan, and the values of the community led to the Salem Witch Trials and the deaths of a number of innocent people. In the case of witch trials, Puritans relied on a variety of different materials, including European texts.

The staunchly religious and moralistic nature of the Puritans has left a lasting legacy far beyond the memories of the Salem Witch Trials. The beliefs about marriage, church and community in the Puritan world continued to impact the United States for much of the 20th century.

SAMPLE LONG ESSAY

The Vietnam War was the most controversial conflict of the 20th century. While World War I and World War II had broad public support, many people questioned the participation in the conflict in Vietnam. While war was never officially declared, the conflict took many American lives and came at a great cost.

The Vietnam War was part of an overall containment strategy on the part of the United States. During the Cold War, the United States operated on the idea that limiting the spread of communism was key, believing that as one nation fell to communism others would, like dominos lined up in a row.

The United States entered the war to stop the spread of communism in East Asia. The United States engaged not only the army of North Vietnam, but also the Viet Cong, a communist guerilla organization in Vietnam. Many in America did not believe the United States should become involved in the conflict, as it did not involve the United States or even a close ally. While the Selective Service had not been particularly troubling to most people during World War II, and many volunteered to serve, Vietnam had far fewer volunteers. Those drafted to fight sometimes refused, fleeing to Canada to avoid the draft.

While U.S. involvement began on a small scale early in the war, it expanded dramatically in 1961 and 1962. Following the Tet Offensive in 1968, American resistance to the war increased significantly. The Tet Offensive was a failed attempt on the part of the communists, but it showed the American people that America was not winning this war. After a substantial investment of money and troops, the United States had made little progress toward victory. In the face of significant resistance from the American public, the United States began a process called Vietnamization, marked by the gradual withdrawal of American troops from Vietnam.

A 1973 peace treaty failed to end the conflict in Vietnam. In April 1975, the North Vietnamese Army captured the city of Saigon, and the nation was reunited under a communist government. There is no question that this was a loss for America. The investment in lives and money had failed, fundamentally, to prevent the spread of communism.

CHAPTER THIRTEEN
Practice Test Two

Multiple-Choice Questions

Read the passage and/or question, and then choose the most correct answer.

Questions 1–5 refer to the following passage.

"The modern states of Latin America and British North America began as overseas colonies of the rising hegemonic nations of Europe; the former by the Spanish and Portuguese, the latter by the English and French... Both the American colonies and the Spanish colonies achieved independence in the late eighteenth and early nineteenth centuries after revolutionary wars. But at this point the similarities stop."

– North, Summerhill and Weingast, *Order, Disorder and Economic Change*, 1999

1. This author wrote "In Defense of the Indians," which condemned Spanish treatment of the Native Americans:
   A. Bartolome de Las Casas
   B. Thomas Hooker
   C. John Winthrop
   D. Opechancanough
   E. Anne Hutchinson

2. He introduced West Indian tobacco to Jamestown and married Pocahontas:
   A. Charles II
   B. Metacom
   C. Arawak
   D. Roger Williams
   E. John Rolfe

3. This Jamestown leader granted a colony in the New World to William Penn:

    A. Anne Hutchinson

    B. John Smith

    C. James Oglethorpe

    D. John Rolfe

    E. Charles II

4. He was a general who established the settlement of Savannah, GA in 1733:

    A. John Winthrop

    B. Opechancanough

    C. Roger Williams

    D. John Smith

    E. James Oglethorpe

5. This Native American leader, nicknamed King Philip by the New Englanders, fought a brutal war against the Puritans:

    A. Metacom

    B. Arawak

    C. Opechancanough

    D. Tecumseh

    E. Pocahontas

Questions 6–9 refer to the following passage.

"For several generations the Puritan lectureships enabled Puritan clergy to propagate their opinions and rally their following. Control of the lectureships gave the laity ecclesiastical power rivaling that of the Crown and the Anglican bishops."

    – Paul Seaver, *The Puritan Lectureships*

6. As the passage above illustrates, lectures and sermons were an integral part of Puritan life. As a leader of the Puritans, this person wrote a famous sermon, "A Model of Christian Charity," with an emphasis on faith and community:

    A. Thomas Hooker

    B. John Winthrop

    C. Anne Hutchinson

    D. John Smith

    E. John Rolfe

7. This person angered Massachusetts' leaders by claiming most ministers were preaching salvation by works rather than by grace, and led religious discussions in his/her own home:

    A. Anne Hutchinson

    B. John Smith

    C. James Oglethorpe

    D. John Rolfe

    E. William Penn

8. This individual organized settlers in Connecticut into a self-governing colony:

    A. Thomas Hooker

    B. John Winthrop

    C. Anne Hutchinson

    D. John Smith

    E. John Rolfe

9. All of the following were powers of royal governors in the colonies, except:

    A. the power to veto assemblies

    B. the power to appoint officials

    C. the power to remove officials

    D. the power to command a militia

    E. the power to print currency

Questions 10 – 15 refer to the following passage.

"When in the Course of human events, it becomes necessary for one people to dissolve the political bands which have connected them with another, and to assume among the powers of the earth, the separate and equal station to which the Laws of Nature and of Nature's God entitle them, a decent respect to the opinions of mankind requires that they should declare the causes which impel them to the separation"

– The Declaration of Independence

10. The purpose of the Declaration of Independence was to:
    A. help New England, which among the colonies, was affected the most with casualties, debt, and depression
    B. explain the role of limited government
    C. explain the necessity of war with Spain
    D. announce the reasons the colonies deserved independence
    E. create a national currency

11. What two groups did the Continental Congress hope to sway with the Declaration of Independence?
    A. the British monarchy and British Parliament
    B. the British monarchy and the French monarchy
    C. Puritans and Quakers in England and America
    D. British citizens and Spanish citizens
    E. the British monarchy and the Spanish monarchy

12. When colonists shouted "no taxation without representation," they were rejecting Parliament's power to:
    A. write every colonial law without input
    B. levy revenue-raising taxes without granting political power
    C. enforce Navigation Laws
    D. regulate trade with Britain
    E. regulate trade with France

13. The Navigation Acts were just a few of the many regulations that angered the colonists. Navigation Laws required all of the following except:
    A. European goods going to the colonies had to first pay duties at an English port
    B. all commerce to and from the colonies could be carried only on English vessels
    C. certain goods produced in the colonies, like tobacco, could only be shipped to England.
    D. the colonies had to develop cloth and iron products manufacturing for themselves
    E. transport of goods to the colonies from British ships and merchants was limited

14. The Proclamation Line of 1763:
    A. exacted burdensome taxes from the colonists to finance Britain's war debts
    B. granted some frontier to Native Americans
    C. prohibited colonists from settling beyond the Appalachian Mountains
    D. made Florida a British territory
    E. made Georgia a British territory

25% DBQ

15. The British turned the tide of the Seven Years' War when they:

    A. defeated the Iroquois allies of the French

    B. pursued William Pitt's policies in North America and elsewhere

    C. convinced the American colonists to share more of the fighting by attacking Quebec on their own

    D. dispatched General Braddock to attack French forts

    E. provided arms to the Native Americans

Questions 16 – 20 refer to the following passage.

"We the People of the United States, in Order to form a more perfect Union, establish Justice, insure domestic Tranquility, provide for the common defense, promote the general Welfare, and secure the Blessings of Liberty to ourselves and our Posterity, do ordain and establish this Constitution for the United States of America."

— The Preamble to the U.S. Constitution

16. This state was the first to ratify the U.S. Constitution:

    A. New York

    B. Rhode Island

    C. Georgia

    D. New Jersey

    E. Delaware

17. How many years is a term of office for a House member?

    A. 2

    B. 4

    C. 6

    D. 3

    E. 8

18. How many years is a term of office for a Senator?

    A. 2

    B. 4

    C. 6

    D. 3

    E. 8

19. Which Amendment states that power not given to the United States or to individual states is reserved for the people?

    A. 1

    B. 2

    C. 5

    D. 7

    E. 10

20. He was a Founding Father who never was President, but was killed by Aaron Burr in a duel:

    A. William Marbury

    B. Alexander Hamilton

    C. William Henry Harrison

    D. Benjamin Franklin

    E. Henry Clay

Questions 21 and 22 refer to the following passage.

"The king of the country where I live hath given me a great province, but I desire to enjoy it with your love and consent, that we may always live together as neighbors and friends...."

— William Penn, *Letter to Native Americans*, 1681

21. This Native American leader united tribes across the country in order to establish an independent nation:

   A. Osceola

   B. Tecumseh

   C. Sequoyah

   D. King Philip

   E. Pocahontas

22. He was a Cherokee leader who promoted peaceful accommodation and created a Cherokee alphabet:

   A. Osceola

   B. Tecumseh

   C. Sequoyah

   D. King Philip

   E. Pocahontas

Questions 23–25 refer to the following passage.

"Every segment of our population, and every individual, has a right to expect from his government a fair deal."

— Harry Truman, 1945

23. What cause championed by the National Organization for Women was passed by Congress, but was never ratified by the states?

   A. Equal Rights Amendment

   B. Mothers against Drunk Driving (MADD)

   C. lower the voting age to 18

   D. eliminating the draft

   E. reinstituting the draft

24. The 1965 Voting Rights Act:

   A. gave naturalized citizens the right to vote

   B. gave women the right to vote

   C. was struck down as unconstitutional by the U.S. Supreme Court

   D. reduced the voting age from 21 to 18

   E. allowed the federal government to enforce voting rights

25. Affirmative action was challenged in the Supreme Court in *Bakke v. UC Board* of Regents due to:

   A. well-qualified applicants were being turned away from the University of California in favor of minority applicants who were not

   B. jobs were unfilled due to minority staffing requirements

   C. international students were given preferential placement over U.S. natural-born citizens.

   D. the university experienced a culture shift as diversity became a large factor

   E. in order to make open courseware more available to all students and release the university from the financial constraints imposed by affirmative action

Questions 26–29 refer to the following passage.

"We stand today on the edge of a New Frontier—the frontier of the 1960's—a frontier of unknown opportunities and perils—a frontier of unfulfilled hopes and threats."

– John F. Kennedy, 1960

26. President Kennedy's domestic policy, "New Frontier..."
    A. expanded U.S. space exploration
    B. allocated funds to find a cure for cancer
    C. was heavily influenced by Cuban domestic policy
    D. looked to lower taxes for the most affluent Americans
    E. focused on reducing poverty and increasing domestic spending

27. The Immigration Act of 1965 did all of the following except:
    A. relieved Cubans seeking to escape the tyranny of Fidel Castro
    B. helped Filipinos seeking economic opportunity
    C. helped people migrate out of the United States
    D. gave foreign nationals a "pathway to citizenship"
    E. opened the nation to foreigners seeking to escape oppression and desiring a new life.

28. The 24th Amendment outlawed:
    A. the poll tax
    B. alcoholic beverages
    C. slavery
    D. income tax
    E. trade with Cuba

29. Under President's Johnson's administration, all of the following programs were born except:
    A. National Endowment for the Humanities
    B. Job Corps
    C. Peace Corps
    D. Department of Transportation
    E. Department of Housing and Urban Development

Questions 30–35 refer to the following passage.

"There are these and other great causes that we were elected overwhelmingly to carry forward in November of 1972. And what we were elected to do, we are going to do, and let others wallow in Watergate, we are going to do our job."

– Richard Nixon, 1973

30. Watergate was:
    A. a hotel holding the Democratic Party National headquarters
    B. an illegal real estate scheme
    C. an illegal gambling operation
    D. a money laundering scheme
    E. none of the above

31. Due to Watergate, President Nixon:
    A. was impeached and acquitted
    B. resigned from office
    C. was pardoned by Gerald Ford
    D. was impeached and forced from office
    E. resigned and was pardoned by Gerald Ford

32. President Nixon's first Vice President Spiro T. Agnew, resigned due to:

    A. indictment on tax evasion and bribery charges; both crimes that took place while he was governor of Maryland

    B. his involvement with the Watergate scandal

    C. drunk driving

    D. allegations that he was involved in voter fraud

    E. indictment on larceny charges

33. Which of the following is not a possible outcome for a federal officer that is convicted in an impeachment case?

    A. Can be exiled from the United States

    B. Can be removed from office

    C. Can be banned from holding future office

    D. Can be tried in court for a related crime

    E. Can undergo impeachment proceedings

34. Woodward and Bernstein were:

    A. two newspaper reporters that investigated Watergate

    B. two FBI agents that investigated Watergate

    C. two Secret Service agents that investigated Watergate

    D. two police officers that investigated Watergate

    E. two cabinet members involved in Watergate

35. In addition to Watergate, President Nixon also faced the challenge of the Vietnam War. His strategy to end the war involved:

    A. bombing Cambodia to close the Ho Chi Minh trail

    B. teaching the South Vietnamese how to fight the war themselves, and withdrawing American troops

    C. seeking support from China

    D. seeking support from the Soviet Union

    E. a joint effort with the United Nations

Questions 36–39 refer to the following passage.

"A recession is when your neighbor loses his job. A depression is when you lose yours. And recovery is when Jimmy Carter loses his."

– Ronald Reagan, 1980

36. Although Carter was criticized for his failures during the U.S. economic crisis of the 1970s, one foreign policy success of his administration was:

    A. the boycott of the 1980 Olympic Games in Moscow

    B. the treaty to relinquish American control of the Panama Canal

    C. averting a second Cuban Missile Crisis

    D. becoming the first U.S. President of the 20th century to visit communist China

    E. improved relations with the Soviet Union

37. President Ronald Reagan selected this nominee for the Supreme Court, whose confirmation was ultimately blocked in the Senate:
    A. Robert Bork
    B. Ruth Bader Ginsberg
    C. Elena Kagan
    D. Warren Burger
    E. Thurgood Marshall

38. Reagan survived an assassination attempt in this year:
    A. 1980
    B. 1982
    C. 1981
    D. 1983
    E. 1987

39. By the year 1999, the World Wide Web brought all of the following into homes in the United States, except for:
    A. shopping
    B. entertainment
    C. Facebook
    D. research websites
    E. business websites

Questions 40 – 45 refer to the following passage.

"They call it Armageddon, the end of freedom as we know it. After I signed the bill, I looked around to see if there were any asteroids falling, some cracks opening up in the earth. Turned out it was a nice day."

– Barack Obama, 2010

40. The above quote came after Obama signed the Patient Protection and Affordable Care Act. This Act guaranteed all of the following except:
    A. health insurance coverage to the previously uninsured
    B. no citizen would be denied coverage due to an inability to pay
    C. no citizen would be denied coverage due to a pre-existing condition
    D. citizens would keep their primary care physicians
    E. policy limits for high cost illnesses would be abolished

41. Many feel that climate change will cause an "Armageddon" of sorts. With evidence of global warming building, world scientists are concerned that:
    A. polar ice cap melting and rising seas will cause mass flooding in major coastal areas
    B. Earth cannot sustain the constant depletion of its natural resources
    C. policies reversed by President Reagan and George H.W. Bush have done irreparable damage to the climate
    D. Europe is surpassing the United States in its efforts to halt dependence on fossil fuels
    E. global governments, much to their detriment, will continue to ignore the seriousness of global warming.

42. Opponents of NAFTA worried that the effects of removing free trade barriers would cause:

   A. loss of American manufacturing jobs

   B. stimulation of the economy

   C. increased global warming

   D. increased emigration from the United States

   E. larger demands on state and local resources

43. The Patriot Act:

   A. permitted the United States to search for weapons of mass destruction

   B. expanded the NSA's powers of surveillance on foreign heads of state

   C. established Guantanamo Bay as a detainment center for terrorist suspects

   D. was written and enacted after the bombing by Timothy McVeigh in Oklahoma City

   E. broadened the government's powers of surveillance

45. Which war/conflict was the first American assault on foreign soil to be brought into the living rooms of Americans by 24/7 cable news?

   A. Operation Desert Storm

   B. Operation Desert Shield

   C. Vietnam War

   D. Korean War

   E. World War II

44. Of the following, which symptom of the "graying of America" will not strain the Social Security system?

   A. the largest segment of the population, the baby boomers, will retire and deplete the assets of the Social Security Trust

   B. baby boomers will continue to retire in larger numbers than there are workers paying into the system through the year 2050

   C. baby boomers will no longer be building up the system at the rate of two or more workers for each retiree

   D. younger workers delay entering the workforce, choosing to go to college instead

   E. by 2030, one-quarter of all Americans drawing on the system will be older than 85

Questions 46–35 refer to the following passage.

"My policy has been…to be upon friendly terms with, but independent of, all the nations of the earth. To share in the broils of none. To fulfil our own engagements. To supply the wants, and be carriers for them all: Being thoroughly convinced that it is our policy and interest to do so."

— George Washington, *Letter to Gouverneur Morris*, 1795

46. All of the following issues were problems with foreign policy in the United States shortly after the Revolutionary War, except:

A. the U.S. Congress was widely respected in Europe

B. the U.S. Congress could not control foreign commerce

C. there were no provisions to protect settlers from Native Americans

D. there were no provisions to repay France for loans made during the Revolutionary Wary

E. there was little trade with Britain

47. George Washington was an Independent, but he was sympathetic towards the Federalists. The following individuals were Anti-Federalists except:

A. Patrick Henry

B. James Monroe

C. John Hancock

D. Alexander Hamilton

E. Samuel Adams

48. Which part of the Federalist program did Jefferson first stop enforcing and then eliminate?

A. Bank of the United States

B. assumption of states' debts

C. funding the debt at par

D. Alien and Sedition Acts

E. Stamp Act

49. Written by John Jay, James Madison, and Alexander Hamilton, this collection of essays attempted to explain to the public how the new U.S. government would work:

A. Bill of Rights

B. Articles of Confederation

C. Federalist Papers

D. Declaration of Independence

E. Constitution

50. The Monroe Doctrine echoes many of the same sentiments as Washington's letter. Monroe attempted to:

A. keep America involved in European conflicts

B. isolate the United States from European intervention in U.S. affairs

C. prevent Europeans from colonizing parts of the West

D. isolate the Western Hemisphere, including both North and South America, from European involvement.

E. increase U.S. involvement in international issues

Questions 51 – 55 refer to the following passage.

"Yes, you need the water. Yes, you need the sun. But that alone won't give you the plant. You need the working hands to give it life."

– Adrian Alvarez

51. 19th century workers organized labor unions for all of the following reasons except:

    A. they were not paid fairly for their work

    B. to overthrow capitalists like Carnegie and Rockefeller

    C. their shifts were frequently 12-14 hours a day

    D. dangerous work conditions

    E. little or no support/assistance for workers injured on the job

52. In 1870, American labor lost overall power to:

    A. a nationwide depression

    B. a nationwide recession

    C. the Great Depression

    D. corporate union-busting tactics

    E. anti-labor legislation passed in the House and Senate

53. By 1900, this union had nearly half a million members:

    A. American Federation of Labor

    B. United Auto Workers

    C. Service Employees International Union

    D. Knights of Labor

    E. National Association for the Advancement of Colored People

54. This President signed the Antiquities Act and designated the first national monument:

    A. Ulysses S. Grant

    B. Theodore Roosevelt

    C. Franklin Roosevelt

    D. Woodrow Wilson

    E. Millard Fillmore

55. This organization advocated for rural mail delivery and price limits on agricultural products and transport:

    A. Colored Farmers' National Alliance

    B. American Federation of Labor

    C. United Farm Workers

    D. the Knights of Labor

    E. the Grange

Short-Answer Questions

Read the passage(s) and question, and then write a short answer arguing your stance.

"This war, if carried on successfully, will have its advantages. We shall drive the British from our continent. They will no longer have an opportunity of intriguing with our Indian neighbors."

– Rep. Felix Grundy, 1811

"The annihilation of our race is at hand unless we unite in one common cause against the common foe. Think not, brave Choctaws and Chickasaws, that you can remain passive and indifferent to the common danger, and thus escape the common fate. Your people, too, will soon be as falling leaves and scattering clouds before their blighting breath. You, too, will be driven away from your native land and ancient domains as leaves are driven before the wintry storms. Sleep not longer, O Choctaws and Chickasaws, in false security and delusive hopes. Our broad domains are fast escaping from our grasp."

– Tecumseh, 1811

1. Based on the above passages, explain the following:
   A. Why did Native Americans fight the United States in the War of 1812?
   B. Explain the results of the War of 1812 in terms of how the United States and Native American groups were affected.

_____
_____
_____
_____
_____
_____
_____
_____
_____
_____
_____
_____
_____
_____
_____
_____
_____
_____
_____
_____
_____
_____

"France is... what they call the dominant power of Europe, being incomparably the most powerful at land, that united in a close alliance with our states, and enjoying the benefit of our trade, there is not the smallest reason to doubt but both will be a sufficient curb upon the naval power of Great Britain."

– Samuel Adams, 1778

2. Based on your knowledge of U.S. history and the above quote, explain the role of France in the American Revolutionary War.

_____
_____
_____
_____
_____
_____
_____
_____
_____
_____
_____
_____
_____
_____
_____
_____
_____

3. Briefly compare the following movements in terms of how they affected social and legal reform in the United States in the 19th century.
    ▶   Abolitionist Movement
    ▶   Women's Rights Movement

_____
_____
_____
_____
_____
_____
_____
_____
_____
_____
_____
_____
_____
_____
_____

4. Briefly explain the Acts of Neutrality and how they changed prior to the bombing of Pearl Harbor.

_____

_____

_____

_____

_____

_____

_____

_____

_____

_____

_____

_____

_____

_____

_____

_____

_____

_____

Document-Based Question

Write an essay using a clearly stated thesis that addresses the question. Use relevant details to support your thesis, derived from your knowledge of U.S. history outside the scope of the documents presented. Your answer should position the argument in a broader, historical context.

Analyze the Temperance Movement, Prohibition, and the growth of organized crime in the United States

DOCUMENT ONE

DOCUMENT TWO

"The prestige of government has undoubtedly been lowered considerably by the prohibition law. For nothing is more destructive of respect for the government and the law of the land than passing laws which cannot be enforced. It is an open secret that the dangerous increase of crime in this country is closely connected with this."

– Albert Einstein, 1921

DOCUMENT THREE

"The use of intoxicating drinks as a beverage is as much an infatuation as is the smoking of opium by the Chinese, and the former is quite as destructive to the success of the business man as the latter."

– P.T. Barnum, 1855

DOCUMENT FOUR

"This American system of ours ... call it Americanism, call it capitalism, call it what you like, gives to each and every one of us a great opportunity if we only seize it with both hands and make the most of it."

– Al Capone, 1930

DOCUMENT FIVE

"Of the demonstrably wise there are but two: those who commit suicide, and those who keep their reasoning faculties atrophied by drink."

– Mark Twain, 1898

DOCUMENT SIX

_____
_____
_____
_____

Long-Essay Question

Write an essay response to the question, using a clear thesis supported by relevant details.

Many historians point to the end of WWII as a critical juncture in the United States truly emerging as a "superpower." Explain what factors led to the United States achieving this title, and explain how the country's stature influenced the Cold War.

Answer Key
MULTIPLE-CHOICE

1.	A	29.	C
2.	E	30.	A
3.	E	31.	D
4.	E	32.	A
5.	A	33.	A
6.	B	34.	A
7.	A	35.	B
8.	A	36.	E
9.	E	37.	A
10.	D	38.	C
11.	A	39.	C
12.	B	40.	D
13.	D	41.	A
14.	C	42.	A
15.	A	43.	E
16.	E	44.	A
17.	A	45.	D
18.	C	46.	A
19.	E	47.	D
20.	B	48.	D
21.	B	49.	C
22.	C	50.	D
23.	A	51.	B
24.	E	52.	A
25.	A	53.	A
26.	E	54.	B
27.	C	55.	E
28.	A		

SAMPLE SHORT ANSWERS

1. Native Americans fought in the War of 1812 to oppose the expansion of the United States into their traditional tribal lands. While the War of 1812 involved the United States and Great Britain, Britain offered arms and support to Native Americans willing to fight the United States in any of several different theaters

of war. While there were various groups involved, a number were organized into Tecumseh's Confederacy in the hopes of establishing a large Indian nation west of the Mississippi River.

2. The assistance of France was critical to the American victory in the Revolutionary War. France provided essential funds, allowing American leaders to supply their troops. French assistance was the result of diplomatic negotiations by Benjamin Franklin. The French also sent troops and skilled military leaders to North America to provide assistance. Without the funds and arms of the French, Britain would have secured an easy victory over the colonists.

3. The women's suffrage and abolitionist movements shared a number of traits and even some activists; however, the abolitionists achieved success much sooner than the suffragettes. Women's suffrage came through political action, with relatively little violence. Abolition came only after the violence of the Civil War. Many in the women's suffrage movement had expected citizenship rights provided in the fourteenth amendment to apply to women, as well as African-Americans. Both abolition and women's suffrage eventually required separate constitutional amendments.

4. The Acts of Neutrality were passed in the 1930s in response to actions taken by Germany in Europe and to the Spanish civil war. These Acts were designed to keep the United States out of the war. The earliest of these Acts limited any support for countries currently at war, disallowing the sale of arms, but allowing the sale of other goods. In the next revision, any trade was disallowed. Later, a cash-and-carry clause allowed the United States to offer some support to Britain and France, but not trade in arms. These restrictions were dropped and after the attack on Pearl Harbor in December, 1941, repealed.

SAMPLE DOCUMENT-BASED ANSWER

Women in the nineteenth century organized, not only for significant political reasons, but also for a moral one. Alcoholism was rampant in nineteenth century America and organizations sprang up across the country to promote temperance. The eventual goal of the temperance movement was prohibition or the criminalization of the sale of alcoholic beverages. The temperance movement was made up largely of religious and rural women, as well as the Anti-Saloon League. Called the *drys*, they blamed alcohol for a number of social issues, including the abandonment of children and families, domestic violence, and poor work behavior. Alcohol consumption was more popular in urban areas with a larger Catholic population.

The temperance movement succeeded and Prohibition became federal law with the passage of the eighteenth amendment to the Constitution. The ownership and consumption of alcohol was not illegal under federal law, and it could still be made for medicinal and religious use. Wine and cider could also be made and consumed at home, although grain-based beer and hard liquor could not be. Alcohol could not be produced commercially, transported, or sold in stores or bars. Some state statutes were more severe, banning ownership or consumption, as well as sale.

This was not a success in many ways. Prohibition did succeed in reducing alcohol consumption significantly, as alcohol became less available and more expensive. In some areas, it created new drinking or non-drinking habits that continued for some time, until the beginning of World War II. While there were Prohibition victories, it failed to stop the sale of alcohol. It simply made sales illegal, creating a new industry—organized crime.

Prohibition and the sale of alcohol funded the growth of organized crime throughout much of the United States. With a significant center in Chicago, these crime networks were money-making enterprises led by powerful men, like the well-known mobster, Al Capone. With that organized crime came the crime boss and significant violence, particularly in major cities. While there had been organized crime on a small scale, for example, managing gambling and prostitution, it had not reached the size and scope of the crime in the 1920s and 1930s until a massive source of money came into play. These criminal networks made their money on the transport and sale of alcohol, bringing in shipments and delivering them to speakeasies or alcohol-serving underground bars. The enforcement of Prohibition was largely inefficient and ineffective and the government was not prepared to manage large organized crime networks.

Prohibition was repealed in 1933. Opponents of Prohibition focused on the class difference. The wealthy retained access to alcohol throughout while the poor were harmed by badly-made moonshine, that often led to illness or death.

SAMPLE LONG ESSAY

After World War II, the United States and the Soviet Union emerged as the two significant world superpowers. While much of the world was ravaged, the United States was economically stronger than ever before, leading to high morale throughout the country. Other countries with political or economic power prior to the war, including Britain, France, and Japan, were significantly weakened. While the United States was doing well, it was now faced with a strong and worrisome ally that had turned into an enemy. The Soviet Union fought alongside the United States during the war, but immediately after the war, began taking measures to consolidate power in Eastern Europe.

The negotiations at the Yalta Conference eventually led to the division of German and Soviet control over Eastern Europe. Western countries were, with U.S. support, re-building democratic governments. The Marshall Plan offered aid to these countries, including West Germany to help them develop strong economies and provide for containment, or the prevention of the spread of communism. The need to contain communism and prevent its spread is a key element in the role of the United States as a military superpower. Furthermore, the United States held a position of power on the United Nations' Security Council, enabling a greater say in world affairs.

With the conflict between the United States and the Soviet Union, the Cold War began, and each of these superpowers had strong militaries. The United States already had the atomic bomb, and the Soviet Union was not far behind; no other country in the world had this capability. Both countries actively worked to increase their military arsenals. They operated with an understanding of massive retaliation, or the idea that an attack would be met with an attack of equal force.

The United States' superpower status was not only due to its economic output and political qualities, but also because of its nuclear weapons. The bombings of Nagasaki and Hiroshima proved that not only could the United States act with extreme military violence, but that it would.

CHAPTER FOURTEEN

Practice Test Three

Multiple-Choice Questions

Read the passage and/or question, and then choose the most correct answer.

Questions 1–5 refer to the following quote.

"America was not willing to chop down the Empire on October 26, 1774, but it was gripping the ax."

– C.L. Gammon, *the Story of the First Continental Congress*

1. Which of the following groups was largely unrepresented at the Constitutional Convention?

   A. Lawyers

   B. Small farmers

   C. Large landowners

   D. Wealthy merchants

   E. Slaves

2. Which city was never a capital of the United States?

   A. Lancaster

   B. Washington, D.C.

   C. Philadelphia

   D. New York City

   E. Pittsburgh

3. Which was not a common argument against ratification of the Constitution?

   A. the President would become too powerful

   B. the states would lose their power

   C. Senators would be elected by state legislatures

   D. a Bill of Rights was not included

   E. there was no religious requirement for holding office

4. The delegates to the Constitutional Convention were influenced by:

   A. faith in direct democracy

   B. distrust of the states

   C. fear of unchecked majorities

   D. belief in compulsory education

   E. none of the above

5. Which decision reached at the Constitutional Convention represented a concession to the South?
   A. taxes on exports were prohibited
   B. the President was to be chosen by an electoral college
   C. revenue bills must originate in the House of Representatives
   D. Congress was given control of interstate commerce
   E. Fugitive Slave Clause

Questions 6 – 9 refer to the following quote.

"The moralities that were followed during our parents' generation were basically arbitrary. This caused a rift between the two generations, which was brought on by the beatniks."

– Peter Fonda

6. Beatniks were characterized by:
   A. volunteering for The Peace Corps
   B. volunteering for the military
   C. rebellion against social norms
   D. vegetarianism
   E. abstinence from alcohol, but overindulgence in narcotics

7. Running counter to the Beatniks, affluence and the rise of the suburbs exploded after WWII. In the 1950s, affluent members of society were encouraged to:
   A. "Keep up with the Joneses"
   B. "Never let them see you sweat"
   C. "Don't let the bastards get you down"
   D. "Fight rather than switch"
   E. "Live to fight another day"

8. What groundbreaking feminist would challenge the "cult of domesticity" in her book, *The Feminine Mystique*?
   A. Gloria Steinem
   B. Gertrude Stein
   C. Betty Friedan
   D. Barbara Ehrenreich
   E. Virginia Woolf

9. This is the name given to Americans born between 1946 and 1964.
   A. Generation X
   B. Generation Y
   C. Millennials
   D. Baby Boomers
   E. Generation B

Questions 10 – 15 refer to the following passage.

"I cannot but hate [indifference for slavery's spread]. I hate it because of the monstrous injustice of slavery itself. I hate it because it deprives our republican example of its just influence in the world—enables the enemies of free institutions, with plausibility, to taunt us as hypocrites—causes the real friends of freedom to doubt our sincerity, and especially because it forces so many really good men amongst ourselves into an open war with the very fundamental principles of civil liberty—criticizing the Declaration of Independence, and insisting that there is no right principle of action but self-interest."

– Abraham Lincoln, 1854

10. The above passage from Lincoln's speech protested what Act?

A. Sherman Anti-Trust Act

B. Kansas-Nebraska Act

C. U.S. Constitution

D. Declaration of Independence

E. Homestead Act

11. This passage from Lincoln's speech would foreshadow a later series of debates in 1858 that would take place between Lincoln and:

A. President Pierce

B. Horace Greely

C. Stephen Douglas

D. Ulysses S. Grant

E. Sam Houston

12. The previous passage would most likely appeal to:

A. pro-slavery advocates

B. Southern politicians

C. abolitionists

D. Stephen Douglas

E. President Pierce

13. What did the Missouri Compromise establish?

A. the border between the slave-owning North and the free South

B. the statehood of Missouri, Maine and Arkansas

C. all states south of Missouri, but not the state of Missouri

D. a boundary that stretched across the 45th parallel

E. the Mason-Dixon line

14. In the Dred Scott Case of 1857, the Supreme Court ruled:

A. African-Americans were not U.S. citizens

B. "separate but equal" was acceptable in public transportation

C. poll taxes were illegal

D. illiteracy tests for voters were illegal

E. African-Americans did not have the right to Social Security

15. This Amendment abolished slavery:

A. fourteenth

B. fifteenth

C. twelvth

D. thirteenth

E. sixteenth

Questions 16 – 18 refer to the following passage.

"What Marxism was to the society of Economic Man, Calvinism was to that of Intellectual Man: the final, messianic exaggeration of its creed. Both abolished actual freedom in existing society to maintain the belief in the reality and imminence of freedom in the coming society. And both collapsed as orders when it was proved that the only society which they could realize was an unfree society."

– Peter F. Drucker, *The End of Economic Man*

16. Which of the following religious groups in America supported the doctrine of predestination?
    A. Church of England
    B. Quaker
    C. Puritan
    D. Orthodox Jewish
    E. Methodist

17. The majority of the writers of the Constitution were:
    A. Puritans
    B. Quakers
    C. Deists
    D. Methodists
    E. Anabaptists

18. The Quakers were another religious group prevalent during early colonial America. Which of the following is/are true about Quakers?
    A. they honored Native American land claims
    B. they were pacifists
    C. they believed in individual religious freedom
    D. all of the above
    E. they believed in abolition

Questions 19 – 23 refer to the following passage.

"We cannot be unmindful that without any design or desire on our part the war has brought us new duties and responsibilities which we must meet and discharge as becomes a great nation, on whose growth and career, from the beginning, the Ruler of Nations had plainly written a high command and pledge of civilization. Incidental to our tenure in the Philippines is the commercial opportunity to which American statesmanship cannot be indifferent."

– William McKinley, 1898

19. In the above quote, McKinley is referencing a war where the United States gained Guam and Puerto Rico as territories. Which war is being referenced?
    A. War of 1812
    B. WWI
    C. WWII
    D. Spanish-American War
    E. The American Revolution

20. What is one reason the United States entered the war mentioned in number 19?
    A. yellow journalism encouraging war in American newspapers
    B. Castro's policies in Cuba
    C. U-boat attacks from Germany
    D. fear of Portuguese attack
    E. desire for land in Asia

21. As a direct result of the war mentioned in number 19, Cuba:
    A. gained independence
    B. became a U.S. territory
    C. temporarily became a U.S. state
    D. became a Communist country
    E. returned to Spanish control

22. These two newspaper publishers are associated with the term *yellow journalism*:

    A. William Randolph Hearst and Joseph Pulitzer

    B. Benjamin Franklin and Joseph Pulitzer

    C. William Randolph Hearst and Rupert Murdoch

    D. Jeff Bezos and Joseph Pulitzer

    E. none of the above

23. Yellow journalism refers to:

    A. journalism that is mostly based on well-researched facts

    B. journalism that is mostly based on sensationalism

    C. journalism that originated with French publications

    D. newspaper journalism

    E. early radio broadcasts

Questions 24–27 refer to the following passage.

"They were careless people, Tom and Daisy they smashed up things and creatures and then retreated back into their money or their vast carelessness or whatever it was that kept them together, and let other people clean up the mess they had made."

– F. Scott Fitzgerald, *The Great Gatsby*

24. Many view Tom and Daisy from *The Great Gatsby* as representative of the recklessness of wealthy investors in the 1920s. The decade crashed to an end on "Black Tuesday," which is the unofficial name for the:

    A. the Wall Street Crash of 1929

    B. the Wall Street Crash of 1987

    C. the Wall Street Crash of 1999

    D. the Wall Street Crash of 2011

    E. the Wall Street Crash of 1939

25. This was the name for women who wore short skirts, listened to jazz, smoked cigarettes in public, and disdained traditional cultural mores:

    A. Victorian women

    B. conservatives

    C. flappers

    D. wet nurses

    E. valley girls

26. The nineteenth amendment was finally ratified during this period, which was a landmark for equal rights in the United States. This amendment granted _____ the right to vote:

    A. citizens 18 or older

    B. women

    C. African-American males

    D. Native Americans

    E. immigrants

27. In the wake of WWI, this President successfully brokered the Washington Arms Conference. Many countries willingly limited their naval power. However, this allowed Japan an opportunity to consolidate power in East Asia.

    A. Coolidge

    B. Lincoln

    C. Eisenhower

    D. Harding

    E. Jefferson

Questions 28 – 32 refer to the following quote.

"Yesterday, December 7, 1941—a date which will live in infamy—the United States of America was suddenly and deliberately attacked by naval and air forces...."

— Franklin D. Roosevelt,
December 8, 1941

28. The attack on Pearl Harbor directly led the United States to:

A. declare war on Japan, effectively entering WWII

B. declare war on Germany, effectively entering WWII

C. declare war on Vietnam, effectively entering the Vietnam Conflict

D. declare war on Japan, effectively entering WWI

E. declare war on both Germany and Japan, entering WWII

29. The "Big Three" were comprised of the following Allied leaders:

A. Hitler, Mussolini, Hirohito

B. Stalin, Roosevelt, Mussolini

C. Stalin, Roosevelt, Churchill

D. Stalin, Churchill, Mussolini

E. Stalin, Mussolini, Hitler

30. After WWII, the Secretary of State proposed to rebuild Europe with the:

A. the use of an atomic device to attack Germany

B. the Marshall Plan

C. that the United States join The League of Nations

D. the Vietnam War

E. the War on Terror

31. During FDR's terms in office, which of the following were created?

A. Tennessee Valley Authority

B. Civilian Conservation Corps

C. Public Works Administration

D. Social Security

E. all of the above

32. To help contain the Soviet Union, Truman created the:

A. Tennessee Valley Authority

B. North American Free Trade Agreement

C. Central Intelligence Agency

D. Social Security

E. Works Progress Administration

Questions 33 – 40 refer to the following quote.

"The arc of the moral universe is long, but it bends toward justice."

— Rev. Martin Luther King, Jr.

33. The notion of "separate but equal" with regards to segregation based on race in public schools was:

A. overturned in the Supreme Court's 1954 decision in *Brown v. Board of Education*.

B. upheld in the Supreme Court's 1954 decision in *Brown v. Board of Education*.

C. used to deny women the right to vote.

D. used to deny African Americans the right to vote.

E. repealed by the nineteenth amendment.

34. The federal government established the authority to monitor state and local elections with:

   A. the Civil Rights Act of 1960

   B. poll taxes

   C. *Brown v. Board of Education*

   D. Voting Rights Act of 1965

   E. Grandfather clauses

35. The Voting Rights Act of 1965:

   A. prohibited denying the right to vote based on the voter's race

   B. made literacy tests illegal

   C. was signed by President John F. Kennedy

   D. allowed the federal government to monitor elections

   E. provided support for voters' rights, including an end to restrictive measures and provisions for enforcement

36. The 1896 Supreme Court decision making "separate but equal" law was:

   A. *Plessy v. Ferguson*

   B. *Brown v. Board of Education*

   C. *Dred Scott v. Sanford*

   D. *Harper v. Virginia Board of Elections*

   E. *Citizens United v. Federal Election Commission*

37. He helped organize the bus boycott in Montgomery, Alabama after Rosa Parks was arrested:

   A. Al Sharpton

   B. Martin Luther King, Jr.

   C. Malcolm X

   D. Jesse Jackson

   E. John Lewis

38. This 1960s civil rights activist was elected to Congress in 1986:

   A. Abbie Hoffman

   B. John Lewis

   C. Jesse Jackson, Jr.

   D. Thurgood Marshall

   E. Rosa Parks

39. He argued *Brown v. Board of Education* and would go on to become the first African-American on the Supreme Court.

   A. Clarence Thomas

   B. Thurgood Marshall

   C. Barack Obama

   D. Booker T. Washington

   E. none of the above

40. This feminist activist founded *Ms. Magazine*:

   A. Susan B. Anthony

   B. Betty Friedan

   C. Audre Lorde

   D. Rosa Parks

   E. Gloria Steinem

Questions 41–44 refer to the following passage.

"Mass death numbs the mind and heart as it numbers its vast toll. Relief from the horror is less possible when we watch old Joe Woods and thirteen-year-old David Shelton plead for life—and then die."

– Phillip Shaw Pauadan, *Victims: A True Story of the Civil War*

41. To promote family farms instead of slave-worked plantations, Congress passed the _____ Act.

A. Homestead

B. Alien and Sedition

C. Postal Service

D. Whiskey

E. Embargo

42. This was the bloodiest single-day battle in U.S. history:

A. Battle of Antietam

B. Battle of Gettysburg

C. First Battle of Bull Run

D. Seven Days' Battle

E. Battle of Fort Sumter

43. The Confederate capital moved from _____ to Richmond, VA:

A. Atlanta, GA

B. Vicksburg, MS

C. Montgomery, AL

D. New Orleans, LA

E. Columbia, SC

44. The Civil War resulted in the South:

A. growing a vibrant economy

B. creating the Federalist Party

C. being economically devastated

D. joining the League of Nations

E. ending its support of racial discrimination

Questions 45 – 50 refer to the following passage.

"To have shrunk, under such circumstances, from manly resistance, would have been a degradation blasting our best and proudest hopes; it would have struck us from the high ranks where the virtuous struggles of our fathers had placed us, and have betrayed the magnificent legacy which we hold in trust for future generations. It would have acknowledged that on the element which forms three-fourths of the globe we inhabit, where all independent nations have equal and common rights, the American people were not an independent people, but colonists and vassals."

– President James Madison address to Congress, November 1812

45. In the War of 1812, the United States fought this European power:

A. Spain

B. France

C. Portugal

D. Canada

E. Britain

46. In 1821, Spain ceded which of these territories to the United States?

A. Florida

B. Rhode Island

C. South Carolina

D. North Carolina

E. Georgia

47. The War of 1812 was ended by the following:

A. Treaty of Paris

B. Treaty of Versailles

C. Treaty of Ghent

D. Yalta Conference

E. The Cold War

48. The Non-Intercourse Act of 1809 disallowed trade with these countries:

- **A.** Spain and France
- **B.** France
- **C.** Portugal and Spain
- **D.** Canada
- **E.** Britain and France

49. He became a hero of the War of 1812 at the Battle of New Orleans:

- **A.** William Marbury
- **B.** George Washington
- **C.** Douglas MacArthur
- **D.** Andrew Jackson
- **E.** Theodore Roosevelt

50. This patriotic song had its origins during the War of 1812:

- **A.** "The Battle Hymn of the Republic"
- **B.** "America the Beautiful"
- **C.** "Stars and Stripes Forever"
- **D.** "The Star-Spangled Banner"
- **E.** none of the above

Questions 51 – 55 refer to the following quote.

"A man who has never gone to school may steal from a freight car; but if he has a university education, he may steal the whole railroad."

– Teddy Roosevelt

51. This historical event made a transnational railroad imperative:

- **A.** the War of 1812
- **B.** the Civil War
- **C.** the Louisiana Purchase
- **D.** World War I
- **E.** the Gilded Age

52. Which of the following is true?

- **A.** The Central Pacific railroad moved from east to west.
- **B.** The Union Pacific railroad moved from north to south.
- **C.** The Union Atlantic railroad moved from west to east.
- **D.** Smaller lines branched east and west from the Central Pacific.
- **E.** none of the above

53. These tent towns, notorious for vice-based businesses, earned this nickname:

- **A.** hell on wheels
- **B.** the end of the line
- **C.** stumptowns
- **D.** shantytowns
- **E.** none of the above

54. This 1882 law, passed after the railroads were completed, banned immigration from which country?

- **A.** China
- **B.** Japan
- **C.** Ireland
- **D.** any Catholic country
- **E.** none of the above

55. The word *millionaire* came into existence with the emergence of this wealthy class:

- **A.** investors
- **B.** railroad tycoons
- **C.** Carnegie fellows
- **D.** congressmen
- **E.** gold prospectors

Short-Answer Questions

Read the passage(s) and question, and then write a short answer arguing your stance.

1. Briefly explain key differences between English and Spanish or French settlements in North America.

_____
_____
_____
_____
_____
_____
_____
_____
_____
_____
_____
_____
_____
_____
_____
_____
_____

"Could I have foreseen what I have, and am like to experience, no consideration upon earth should have induced me to accept this command."

– George Washington, 1775

"If we separate from Britain, what code of laws will be established? How shall we be governed so as to retain our liberties? Can any government be free which is not administered by general stated laws? Who shall frame these laws? Who will give them force and energy?"

– Abigail Adams, 1775

2. Based on your knowledge of U.S. history and the above quotes, what specific measures did American colonists take to establish a new government?

_____
_____
_____
_____
_____
_____
_____
_____
_____
_____

_____
_____
_____
_____
_____

3. Compare any two of the following wars and briefly explain how they helped shape the United States:

   ▶ Civil War

   ▶ Spanish-American War

   ▶ the War of 1812

   ▶ the Global War on Terror

   ▶ World War II

_____
_____
_____
_____
_____
_____
_____
_____
_____
_____
_____
_____
_____
_____
_____

4. Briefly explain why the United States was unsuccessful in ratifying the Treaty of Versailles.

_____
_____
_____
_____
_____
_____
_____
_____
_____
_____
_____
_____
_____
_____
_____

Document-Based Question

Write an essay using a clearly stated thesis that addresses the question. Use relevant details to support your thesis, derived from your knowledge of U.S. history outside the scope of the documents presented. Your answer should position the argument in a broader, historical context.

Analyze slavery in the United States, including major slave revolts, the Abolitionist Movement, and the argument of slavery as a cause of the American Civil War.

DOCUMENT ONE

DOCUMENT TWO

My Lords,

I beg leave to lay before your Lordships an account of our Affairs, first in regard to the Desertion of our Negroes... On the 9th of September last at Night a great Number of Negroes Arose in Rebellion, broke open a Store where they got arms, killed twenty one White Persons, and were marching the next morning in a Daring manner out of the Province, killing all they met and burning several Houses as they passed along the Road. I was returning from Granville County with four Gentlemen and met these Rebels at eleven o'clock in the forenoon and fortunately discerned the approaching danger time enough to avoid it, and to give notice to the Militia who on the Occasion behaved with so much expedition and bravery, as by four o'clock the same day to come up with them and killed and took so many as put a stop to any further mischief at that time, forty-four of them have been killed and Executed; some few yet remain concealed in the Woods expecting the same fate, seem desperate...

It was the Opinion of His Majesty's Council with several other Gentlemen that one of the most effectual means that could be used at present to prevent such desertion of our Negroes is to encourage some Indians by a suitable reward to pursue and if possible to bring back the Deserters, and while the Indians are thus employed they would be in the way ready to intercept others that might attempt to follow and I have sent for the Chiefs of the Chickasaws living at New Windsor and the Catawbaw Indians for that purpose. . . .

My Lords,

Your Lordships Most Obedient and Most Humble Servant

Wm Bull

– Lieutenant Governor William Bull of South Carolina, 1739

DOCUMENT THREE

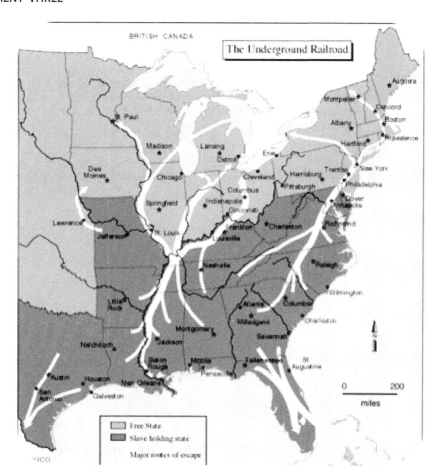

DOCUMENT FOUR

"On the first day of January, in the year of our Lord one thousand eight hundred and sixty-three, all persons held as slaves within any State or designated part of a State, the people whereof shall then be in rebellion against the United States, shall be then, thenceforward, and forever free; and the Executive Government of the United States, including the military and naval authority thereof, will recognize and maintain the freedom of such persons, and will do no act or acts to repress such persons, or any of them, in any efforts they may make for their actual freedom."

– from the Emancipation Proclamation, 1863

DOCUMENT FIVE

DOCUMENT SIX

Long-Essay Question

Write an essay response to the question using a clear thesis supported by relevant details.

Explain how the U.S. policy of isolationism, as explained in the Monroe Doctrine, played out in U.S. foreign policy until the end of the 19th century.

_____
_____
_____
_____
_____
_____
_____
_____
_____
_____
_____
_____
_____
_____
_____
_____
_____
_____
_____
_____
_____
_____
_____
_____
_____
_____
_____
_____
_____
_____
_____
_____
_____
_____
_____
_____
_____
_____
_____
_____
_____

Answer Key
MULTIPLE-CHOICE

1.	E	29.	C
2.	E	30.	B
3.	E	31.	E
4.	C	32.	C
5.	E	33.	A
6.	C	34.	A
7.	A	35.	E
8.	C	36.	A
9.	D	37.	B
10.	B	38.	B
11.	C	39.	B
12.	C	40.	E
13.	E	41.	A
14.	A	42.	A
15.	D	43.	C
16.	C	44.	C
17.	C	45.	E
18.	E	46.	A
19.	D	47.	C
20.	A	48.	E
21.	A	49.	D
22.	A	50.	D
23.	B	51.	B
24.	A	52.	E
25.	C	53.	A
26.	B	54.	A
27.	D	55.	B
28.	A		

SAMPLE SHORT ANSWERS

1. One of the most significant differences between English and Spanish or French settlements in North America was the relationship between the settlers and Native Americans. The English typically settled as families, with their wives and children, whereas it was common for single Spanish and French men to

ocal women and build families in the New World. While
ench treatment of native peoples was not consistently positive, it
only violent, largely because of these relationships.

States recognized the need for a government built around laws,
aws had to be acceptable to the people. Enlightenment principles
government was a contract between the individual and society. Large
tions provided voices for various groups, while the Bill of Rights and a
n of checks and balances prevented concentrated governmental power and
uption.

3. The Spanish-American war of the 1890s and the War in Iraq and Afghanistan
    are each the result of American intervention. In the Spanish-American War,
    the United States entered the Cuban War for Independence. In Iraq and
    Afghanistan, the United States entered with the goal of deposing ruling
    governments as part of the War on Terror. In some ways, these two shared
    a common aim. In both cases, the United States wanted to gain additional
    control over other regions of the world and to spread their influence. The Span-
    ish-American War helped the United States gain influence in the Caribbean
    and Latin America, but the wars in Iraq and Afghanistan created regional
    instability and fostered increased resistance to U.S. goals in the Muslim world.
    Both wars also revived American militarism, ending periods of relative peace.

4. While the United States had played a key role in World War I, it failed to ratify
    the Treaty of Versailles that ended the war. While U.S. President Woodrow
    Wilson supported the Treaty, the Senate (particularly Senator Henry Cabot
    Lodge) did not. Many different groups within Europe disapproved of the terms
    of the treaty, including German-Americans, Italian-Americans, and even
    Irish-Americans. The failure of the United States to sign and to join the League
    of Nations would have disastrous consequences in coming years.

SAMPLE DOCUMENT-BASED ANSWERS

The practice of chattel slavery in the United States dates to relatively early in colonial
history. As early as the Constitutional Convention, some people, particularly in the
North, were expressing discomfort with the institution of slavery. The abolitionist
movement grew throughout the first half of the nineteenth century, eventually culmi-
nating in the thirteenth amendment, which ended slavery.

Prior to the colonization of North America, slaves worked sugar plantations in the
Caribbean, and soon plantation agriculture was used in the southern states to farm
cotton and tobacco. Plantation agriculture required large numbers of workers, and
slaves were considered ideal for this purpose. They had no legal rights, required no
payment, and increased in number through natural reproduction. The institution of
slavery was, to the colonists of the early eighteenth century, a practical business choice.

Conditions for slaves remained relatively constant through much of this period, with occasional slave rebellions or revolts. These revolts led to short-term violence, but no lasting improvements or freedoms. Relatively few people owned large numbers of slaves, and many owned none at all.

The framers of the U.S. Constitution agreed that the importation of slaves would end in 1807; however, this did not end the slave trade. Slaves were still bought and sold, typically at auction. The Constitution also included the Fugitive Slave Act, limiting the ability of slaves to run away and make it to freedom. These measures were compromises between northerners, who were less comfortable with slavery, and southern states, who wished to preserve it. Later compromises included the Missouri Compromise and the Kansas-Nebraska Act. Eventually all of these failed and the nation fell into Civil War.

The abolitionists actively condemned slavery as inhumane and unacceptable. Abolitionists wanted slavery banned, and some advocated for equality among the races. Many abolitionists were Quakers, who had condemned slavery as early as the seventeenth century. Abolitionism grew substantially with the publication of various books, including works by Harriet Tubman and Frederick Douglass. These were heavily circulated and read, leading to broad support for the abolition of slavery. By the time of the Civil War, the Republican Party had embraced abolition.

Slavery came to an end with the victory of the Union in the Civil War. Lincoln issued the Emancipation Proclamation during the war. This was followed by the thirteenth amendment ending slavery, as well as the fourteenth amendment, providing African-Americans with citizenship in the United States. The fight for civil rights was far from over, but for a brief period after the war and before the *Plessy v. Ferguson* decision, African-Americans enjoyed a new level of freedom and community support as they moved from slavery to life as free citizens.

SAMPLE LONG ESSAY

The Monroe Doctrine, crafted in 1823, defined U.S. foreign policy throughout the nineteenth century. Designed to isolate the United States from international affairs while protecting itself from colonization efforts, the Monroe Doctrine was a success. Later politicians, well into the twentieth century, cited the Monroe Doctrine to justify their political decisions or actions.

Around the time the Monroe Doctrine was written, many Latin American countries were newly freed from colonial European powers, including Spain and Portugal. By 1825, Spain still controlled Cuba and Puerto Rico, but nothing more. There were several goals of the Monroe Doctrine. First and foremost, the United States, along with Britain, wanted to prevent any future European colonization of North or South America. The Monroe Doctrine stated this in clear terms, as well as committing to non-involvement in any European disputes. The United States promised not to interfere with existing colonies, but also to defend newly independent nations in the western hemisphere. Essentially, this doctrine declared that any intervention in North, Central, or South America would and could be met with action, but that the United States would not take action outside of those terms.

While the Monroe Doctrine was an American political plan, it was created with the full support of Britain who provided the naval forces to enforce it for several years. This relationship, after some challenges, evolved into the "special relationship" that the United States and Britain shared throughout the nineteenth and twentieth centuries. The Monroe Doctrine was well received by Latin American countries, who viewed the protection of Britain as a benefit. While the nations of North and South America never united to take political action together, they did meet and maintain diplomatic relations.

By the 1840s, the Monroe Doctrine was used to justify expansionism, into not only the western states of the country, but Hawaii as well. The Doctrine was challenged when Napoleon III invaded and conquered Mexico; however, his emperor had been executed before the U.S. Civil War came to an end. The Monroe Doctrine was used to justify other actions, including the Spanish-American War. During the Cold War, the Monroe Doctrine provided the basis for providing aid to Latin American countries to prevent the spread of communism.

The Monroe Doctrine provided the United States with justifications for both isolationism and when needed, interference. It protected the United States from colonization, as well as many conflicts in Europe. The United States was even able to stay out of both World War I and World War II until directly exposed to a threat.

CHAPTER FIFTEEN
Practice Test Four

Multiple-Choice Questions

Read the passage and/or question, and then choose the most correct answer.

1. This all-black Army fighter plane squadron fought in the skies over North Africa.

   A. the Blue Tails

   B. the Red Barons

   C. the Tuskegee Airmen

   D. there were no all-black fighter plane squadrons

   E. none of the above

2. By serving four terms, FDR earned this nickname:

   A. "Old Hickory"

   B. "Handsome Frank"

   C. "His Obstinacy"

   D. "The King of America"

   E. "The Gipper"

3. Before FDR's four terms and the passage of the twenty-second amendment, why had no previous president exceeded two terms in the White House?

   A. they all lost their bids for reelection

   B. most Presidents died in office before their third term

   C. it was an unofficial custom based on Washington's two terms

   D. the Supreme Court prevented Presidents from sitting too long

   E. the job was so stressful that no one wanted it beyond eight years

Questions 4 and 5 refer to the following passage.

"We came back to Los Angeles at the end of the war, believing that there was no other way but to be American. We were discouraged with our Japanese culture. My feeling at the time was, I had to prove myself. I don't know why I had to prove myself. Here I am, an ex-GI, born and raised here. Why do I have to prove myself? We all had this feeling. We had to prove that we were Americans."

– Peter Ota, an interned Japanese-American veteran

4. Why did America intern Japanese-Americans in World War II?
   A. because of proven security risks from Japanese citizens.
   B. to provide protection to Japanese-Americans
   C. the United States questioned the loyalty of Japanese-Americans
   D. to eliminate the risk of Japanese-Americans returning to Japan
   E. because Japanese-Americans lived primarily in large cities

5. What were internment's lasting effects on Japanese-Americans?
   A. the government immediately compensated them
   B. they were not compensated at all
   C. many lost their property and were treated as potential traitors
   D. they were forcibly relocated to the East Coast
   E. there were no lasting effects

6. Japan surrendered after 200,000 Japanese civilians were killed by:
   A. the Firebombing of Tokyo
   B. the Battle of Iwo Jima
   C. two atomic bombs
   D. the Marines
   E. the Chinese Red Army

7. Which U.S. President authorized $20,000 reparation payments to each interned Japanese-American individual?
   A. George H. W. Bush
   B. Ronald Reagan
   C. George W. Bush
   D. Gerald Ford
   E. Franklin Roosevelt

8. Which President desegregated the Armed Forces?
   A. Franklin Roosevelt
   B. Dwight D. Eisenhower
   C. Harry S. Truman
   D. John F. Kennedy
   E. Bill Clinton

9. This U.S. Secretary of State created a plan to rebuild Europe:
   A. Henry Kissinger
   B. James Baker
   C. Madeleine Albright
   D. George Marshall
   E. George Schultz

10. What directly led to the entry of the United States into World War II?
    A. the sinking of the *Lusitania*
    B. Nazi human rights atrocities
    C. Britain's need for assistance
    D. the attack on Pearl Harbor
    E. the assassination of Franz Ferdinand

Questions 11 – 14 refer to the following quote.

"He that will not work shall not eat."

– John Smith, 1607

11. Which was not a factor in Jamestown's disastrous first few years?
    A. lack of food that led to starvation
    B. unwillingness of the organizers to risk further expenses
    C. diseases that the colonists could not treat or prevent
    D. conflict between the colonists and local natives
    E. lack of skills that made it impossible to create necessary goods

12. This group established the Jamestown Colony:
    A. Church of England
    B. Virginia Trading Company
    C. British Parliament
    D. the Puritans
    E. the Quakers

13. This group of tribal nations, from whom Pocahontas hailed, alternately fought with and aided the Jamestown settlers:
    A. Algonquin
    B. Iroquois Nation
    C. Sioux Confederacy
    D. Powhatan
    E. Paspahegh

14. In contrast to Jamestown, the colony of Savannah:
    A. instituted religiously tolerant policies
    B. failed and was abandoned in the seventeenth century
    C. was a Spanish colony
    D. was all-male
    E. had no casualties for the first twenty-five years

Questions 15 and 16 refer to the following quote.

"Thus far, impress'd by New England writers and schoolmasters, we tacitly abandon ourselves to the notion that our United States has been fashion'd from the British Islands only, and essentially form a second England only—which is a very great mistake."

– Walt Whitman, 1883

15. Whitman alludes to Spanish influence in North America—what was Spain's primary motivation for establishing colonies?
    A. to develop commercial enterprises
    B. to convert Native Americans
    C. to develop defensive borders that would protect its more lucrative trading empire in Mexico and Peru
    D. to keep the English out of the area
    E. to keep the French out of the area

16. England was not overly interested in establishing colonies in North America for most of the sixteenth century because:
    A. They did not have a strong military.
    B. They thought the world was flat.
    C. They felt they should establish more colonies in Africa before going to a different continent.
    D. The government was under the strain of internal problems.
    E. They did not believe North America had resources they could use.

17. All of these factors contributed to the destruction of native populations in North America except:
    A. the unintentional transfer of smallpox from Europeans to Native Americans
    B. Europeans using infected blankets as biological weapons of war
    C. large-scale Spanish enslavement of tribes
    D. constant battle with Europeans over territory and resources
    E. geographical displacement by colonists

18. This Native American city, near modern-day St. Louis, was as large as London or Venice in the year 1250:
    A. Teotihuacan
    B. Acoma Pueblo
    C. Cahokia
    D. Mesa Verde
    E. Machu Picchu

19. The Treaty of Tordesillas, signed in 1494, divided the New World between which European nations?
    A. Portugal and Spain
    B. Portugal and England
    C. Portugal and France
    D. England and Spain
    E. none of the above

Question 20 refers to the following passage.

"If any slave who shall be out of the house or plantation where such slave shall live or shall be usually employed, or without some white person in company with such slave, shall refuse to submit or to undergo the examination of any white person, it shall be lawful for any such white Person to pursue, apprehend and moderately correct such slave; and if such slave shall assault and strike such white person, such slave may be lawfully killed."

– South Carolina Slave Code, 1740

20. The Slave Code was written as a result of:
    A. The Stono Rebellion
    B. John Brown's raid on Harper's Ferry
    C. Nat Turner's insurrection
    D. Denmark Vesey's thwarted insurrection
    E. none of the above

21. From the mid-1600s to the mid-1700s, anywhere from fifty to sixty-five percent of European immigrants in the American colonies were:

A. members of English aristocracy

B. physicians

C. searching for gold

D. indentured servants

E. none of the above

22. The Stono Rebellion:

A. was an uprising of poor Virginia farmers in the early 1700s

B. caused an increase in whiskey tariffs after the Revolution

C. was an uprising where slaves in South Carolina attempted to reach Spanish-controlled Florida to gain independence

D. was crushed by Dutch mercenaries

E. led to the Fugitive Slave Act

23. All of these were factors in the rise of slavery in British colonies except:

A. ample land for agricultural activity

B. a lack of indentured servants

C. the growing popularity of Quakerism

D. the inability to successfully enslave Native Americans

E. growing demand for colonial goods such as tobacco

24. "Remember the *Maine*" became a rallying cry for many Americans during the Spanish-American War. The *Maine* was:

A. sunk by a Spanish U-Boat

B. sunk by a German U-Boat

C. a ship that mysteriously exploded near Cuba

D. a ship was sunk by the Japanese in Cuba

E. none of the above

25. After the Spanish-American War, the United States gained the following territories:

A. Puerto Rico, Philippines, Guam

B. Cuba, Philippines, Guam

C. Puerto Rico, Cuba, Guam

D. Philippines, Guam, Panama

E. Philippines, Guam, the Bahamas

26. President Taft's policy of combined private and public investment in foreign countries to increase American influence was known as:

A. *quid pro quo*

B. the Roosevelt Corollary

C. Manifest Destiny

D. soft power

E. dollar diplomacy

27. Early in the twentieth century, U.S. military action led to the creation of a new Constitution and the election of Venustiano Carraza in which Latin American country?

A. Puerto Rico

B. Nicaragua

C. Cuba

D. Mexico

E. Panama

28. This hero of the Spanish-American War went on to become the nation's twenty-sixth President.

A. George Washington

B. Thomas Jefferson

C. Theodore Roosevelt

D. Franklin Roosevelt

E. Ulysses S. Grant

29. World War I was ended by:
- **A.** a peace treaty drafted by the League of Nations
- **B.** the Treaty of Versailles
- **C.** NATO
- **D.** the United Nations
- **E.** none of the above

30. The *Lusitania* was a British luxury liner that was sunk by:
- **A.** an iceberg
- **B.** Spanish saboteurs in Cuba
- **C.** German submarines (U-Boats)
- **D.** Italian U-Boats
- **E.** Japanese kamikazes

31. The Zimmerman telegram:
- **A.** contained a promise that Germany would help Mexico receive lost territories if Mexico declared war against the United States
- **B.** was a catalyst in causing the United States to enter World War I
- **C.** was a catalyst in causing the United States to refuse to enter World War I
- **D.** A and B
- **E.** A and C

32. After World War I, the United States:
- **A.** did not join the League of Nations
- **B.** joined the League of Nations
- **C.** ratified the Treaty of Versailles
- **D.** refused to ratify the Treaty of Versailles
- **E.** created the League of Nations

33. He was President during World War I:
- **A.** Theodore Roosevelt
- **B.** Franklin Roosevelt
- **C.** Harry S. Truman
- **D.** B and C
- **E.** Woodrow Wilson

34. Upon receipt of the Zimmerman Telegram, Mexico:
- **A.** Immediately declared war on the United States
- **B.** ignored it and eventually rejected it, remaining neutral in World War I
- **C.** quickly warned the United States of Germany's impending attack
- **D.** declared war on Germany
- **E.** none of the above

35. In which period did J.P. Morgan make his fortune?
- **A.** The New Deal
- **B.** The Gilded Age
- **C.** The Industrial Revolution
- **D.** World War II
- **E.** World War I

36. Andrew Carnegie is well-known for his belief that:
- **A.** The very wealthy deserved their wealth
- **B.** The very wealthy had a responsibility to redistribute wealth
- **C.** The very wealthy should gain control of resources
- **D.** Trusts generated additional wealth
- **E.** Trusts should be legally regulated

37. Morgan was:
    A. a banker
    B. an oil tycoon
    C. a coal tycoon
    D. a steel tycoon
    E. a land developer

38. Anti-Trust legislation was designed to:
    A. reduce wealth
    B. redistribute wealth
    C. prevent price controls
    D. stop businesses from expanding to a very large size
    E. prevent buyouts and conglomerations

39. Which of the following families is not connected to the wealth of the Gilded Era?
    A. J.P. Morgan
    B. Andrew Carnegie
    C. John D. Rockefeller
    D. John F. Kennedy
    E. all of the above became wealthy in the Gilded Era

Questions 40 and 41 refer to the following passage.

There surged around me an evil-smelling stink, men and boys reached out to touch me. They were in rags and the remnants of uniforms. Death already had marked many of them, but they were smiling with their eyes. I looked out over the mass of men to the green fields beyond, where well-fed Germans were ploughing...

                                    – Edward R. Murrow

40. Murrow's radio reports on this event illustrated the horrors of the Holocaust for American listeners:
    A. World War II
    B. World War I
    C. the Nuremberg Trials
    D. the use of the atom bomb
    E. Selective Service

41. The Nuremberg Trials prosecuted what?
    A. using weapons of mass destruction
    B. genocide
    C. violation of international borders
    D. treatment of prisoners of war
    E. war crimes

42. Tensions in the Cold War peaked with this incident:
    A. Korean War
    B. Vietnam War
    C. Bay of Pigs
    D. Battle of the Bulge
    E. Perestroika

43. In 1950, the United States entered this conflict:
    A. World War II
    B. Vietnam War
    C. Korean War
    D. Global War on Terror
    E. Cold War

44. The Vietnam War extended beyond its official end in 1973, until:
    A. the fall of Saigon
    B. the Tet Offensive
    C. the Gulf of Tonkin Incident
    D. the Viet Cong were defeated
    E. the Battle of Ap Bac

45. In 1956, the United States supported the Israeli invasion of Egypt in:
   A. the Suez Crisis
   B. the Six-Day War
   C. the First Arab-Israeli War
   D. the Yom Kippur War
   E. the First Intifada

46. This Reagan-era program, nicknamed "Star Wars," was designed to end the policy of massive retaliation during the Cold War:
   A. Space Defense Institute
   B. Strategic Defense Institute
   C. Space Defense Initiative
   D. Strategic Defense Initiative
   E. none of the above

47. Before the United States invaded, Afghanistan was ruled by:
   A. the Northern Alliance
   B. the Taliban
   C. Al-Qaeda
   D. ISIS
   E. Pakistan

48. Current economic policy debate surrounds all of these issues except:
   A. job creation
   B. deficit reduction
   C. inflation
   D. deflation
   E. health care reform

49. Illegal immigration from Mexico to the United States has given rise to:
   A. U.S. plans to invade Central America
   B. human rights abuses by organized criminal groups
   C. a policy of amnesty for all undocumented immigrants
   D. decreased border security
   E. a wave of pro-immigrant sentiment in American politics

50. This conservative activist fought the ERA through her organization, the Eagle Forum:
   A. Gloria Steinem
   B. Phyllis Schlafly
   C. Betty Friedan
   D. Susan Faludi
   E. Naomi Klein

51. This economic policy allows companies to set both prices and wages as they see fit, without government interference:
   A. anarchism
   B. socialism
   C. progressivism
   D. mercantilism
   E. *lassez-faire*

52. This law reduced the ability of railroads to create monopolies and set prices without market interference:
   A. Anti-Trust Act
   B. International Commerce Act
   C. Interstate Commerce Act
   D. tenth amendment
   E. none of the above

53. This Progressive believed that wealth accumulated by owning land and resources was the main cause of poverty:

   A. Henry George

   B. Teddy Roosevelt

   C. Eugene Debs

   D. Jane Addams

   E. Louis Brandeis

54. This religious organization sought to apply Christian ethics to issues of social justice during the Gilded Age:

   A. the Catholic Church

   B. the Liberation Theologians

   C. the Social Gospel

   D. the New Puritans

   E. none of the above

55. American socialists advocated for:

   A. an eight-hour workday

   B. a five-day workweek

   C. an end to competition

   D. state ownership of resources

   E. all of the above

Short-Answer Questions

Read the passage(s) and question, and then write a short answer arguing your stance.

1. Compare or contrast the following:
   ▶ reasons the United States entered World War I
   ▶ reasons United States entered World War II.

_____
_____
_____
_____
_____
_____
_____
_____
_____
_____
_____
_____
_____
_____
_____
_____
_____
_____

"Racial segregation must be seen for what it is — and that is an evil system, a new form of slavery covered up with certain niceties of complexity."

– Martin Luther King Jr.

2. Based on your knowledge of U.S. history and the above quote, briefly explain ONE of the following:
   A. Compare the Civil Rights Movement of the 1950s and 1960s to the Abolitionist Movement prior to the American Civil War.
   B. Compare Jim Crow laws of the American South of the late 19th and 20th century to the Black Codes of the American South prior to the American Civil War.

_____
_____
_____
_____
_____
_____
_____
_____
_____
_____
_____

_____
_____
_____
_____

3. Compare any two of the following and explain how they helped shape the United States.

   ▶ the nineteenth amendment
   ▶ the fifteenth amendment
   ▶ the twenty-sixth amendment
   ▶ the eighteenth amendment
   ▶ the twenty-first amendment

_____
_____
_____
_____
_____
_____
_____
_____
_____
_____
_____
_____
_____
_____

4. Briefly explain key differences between Quakers and Puritans, including political and religious views.

_____
_____
_____
_____
_____
_____
_____
_____
_____
_____
_____
_____
_____
_____
_____

Document-Based Questions

Write an essay using a clearly stated thesis that addresses the question. Use relevant details to support your thesis, derived from your knowledge of U.S. history outside the score of the documents presented. Finally, your answer should position the argument in a broader, historical context.

Explain the role of the public in supporting U.S. efforts during World War II.

DOCUMENT ONE

"Soldiers, Sailors and Airmen of the Allied Expeditionary Forces: You are about to embark upon the Great Crusade, toward which we have striven these many months. The eyes of the world are upon you. The hopes and prayers of liberty-loving people everywhere march with you. In company with our brave Allies and brothers-in-arms on other Fronts you will bring about the destruction of the German war machine, the elimination of Nazi tyranny over oppressed peoples of Europe, and security for ourselves in a free world. Your task will not be an easy one. Your enemy is well trained, well equipped and battle-hardened. He will fight savagely. But this is the year 1944. Much has happened since the Nazi triumphs of 1940-41. The United Nations have inflicted upon the Germans great defeats, in open battle, man-to-man. Our air offensive has seriously reduced their strength in the air and their capacity to wage war on the ground. Our Home Fronts have given us an overwhelming superiority in weapons and munitions of war, and placed at our disposal great reserves of trained fighting men. The tide has turned. The free men of the world are marching together to victory. I have full confidence in your courage, devotion to duty, and skill in battle. We will accept nothing less than full victory. Good Luck! And let us all beseech the blessing of Almighty God upon this great and noble undertaking."

– Dwight Eisenhower, speech to troops on D-Day, 1941

DOCUMENT TWO

He was a famous trumpet man from out Chicago way

He had a boogie style that no one else could play

He was the top man at his craft

But then his number came up and he was gone with the draft

He's in the army now, a-blowin' reveille

He's the boogie woogie bugle boy of Company B

They made him blow a bugle for his Uncle Sam

It really brought him down because he couldn't jam

The captain seemed to understand

Because the next day the cap' went out and drafted a band

And now the company jumps when he plays reveille

He's the boogie woogie bugle boy of Company B

> – "Boogie Woogie Bugle Boy," The Andrews Sisters, 1941

DOCUMENT THREE

DOCUMENT FOUR

DOCUMENT FIVE

"We call upon the president and congress to declare war on Japan and racial prejudice in our country. Certainly we should be strong enough to whip them both."

– The Pittsburg Courier, December 13, 1941

DOCUMENT SIX

"My own opinion was that blacks could best overcome racist attitudes through their achievements, even though these had to take place within the hateful environment of segregation....We owned a fighter squadron — something that would have been unthinkable only a short time earlier. It was all ours... Furthermore, we would be required to analyze our own problems and solve them with our own skills."

– Benjamin O. Davis, first African American Air Force General, 1942

Long-Essay Question

Write an essay response to the question, using a clear thesis supported by relevant details.

Some historians posit that President Franklin Roosevelt's "New Deal" was socialist in nature. Support or refute this claim citing specific New Deal programs.

_____
_____
_____
_____
_____
_____
_____
_____
_____
_____
_____
_____
_____
_____
_____
_____
_____
_____
_____
_____
_____
_____
_____
_____
_____
_____
_____
_____
_____
_____
_____
_____
_____
_____
_____
_____
_____
_____
_____
_____
_____
_____

Answer Key
MULTIPLE-CHOICE

1.	C	**29.**	B
2.	D	**30.**	D
3.	C	**31.**	A
4.	B	**32.**	E
5.	C	**33.**	A
6.	C	**34.**	B
7.	B	**35.**	C
8.	C	**36.**	B
9.	D	**37.**	A
10.	D	**38.**	D
11.	B	**39.**	E
12.	B	**40.**	C
13.	D	**41.**	E
14.	A	**42.**	C
15.	C	**43.**	C
16.	D	**44.**	A
17.	B	**45.**	A
18.	C	**46.**	D
19.	A	**47.**	B
20.	A	**48.**	D
21.	D	**49.**	B
22.	C	**50.**	B
23.	C	**51.**	E
24.	C	**52.**	C
25.	A	**53.**	A
26.	E	**54.**	C
27.	D	**55.**	E
28.	C		

SAMPLE SHORT ANSWERS

1. The United States, while concerned about the war and engaging diplomatically, did not enter World War I until 1917, after the Zimmerman telegraph was intercepted. This text stated that Germany was prepared to offer aid to Mexico to retake Texas. With a clear threat that involved the United States, at last,

the United States was prepared to enter the war. In World War II, it was not a threat but a direct attack that brought the United States into the war. When Japan bombed Pearl Harbor in December 1941, the United States entered the war at once. Hitler's declaration of war followed at once.

2. Both the abolitionist movement and the Civil Rights movement worked to achieve specific goals for African Americans. The abolitionist movement was focused on the end of slavery. Noted abolitionists were sometimes former slaves, but others were Quakers or northern pastors. Abolitionists focused on a single specific issue, the abolition of slavery. Civil Rights activists dealt with a much wider range of issues, including voting rights, segregation and widespread discrimination. Religious individuals, including pastors of traditionally African-American churches played an essential role once again. In both movements, strong African-American orators played a key role; however, within the Civil Rights movement, there was an additional possibility for political power in the Congress, Senate or judiciary.

3. Both the 18th Amendment and the 19th Amendment were the result of the work of women. Women in the temperance and suffrage movements worked to influence pastors and politicians to achieve significant social change. Their goals, were, in some ways, similar. Both viewed their movements as a way to improve the lives and lot of women in American society. Notably, Prohibition passed earlier than women's suffrage. Women's suffrage was applied equally across society, while Prohibition had the strongest effect on the lower classes. The 19th Amendment has remained unchallenged, while the 18th is the only constitutional amendment ever repealed.

4. Both the Quakers and the Puritans are religious groups founded after the Protestant Reformation. These two groups were remarkably different in their religious beliefs and practices. The Puritans were focused on a highly structured society, with obedience to church and community at the center of their belief system. The Quakers believed in a direct, personal and individual relationship with God. Women were treated as relative equals, and the Quakers were active in the abolitionist movement. For Quakers, morality, peace, and individual behavior were key.

SAMPLE DOCUMENT-BASED ANSWERS

World War II brought America together in an attempt to support the war effort. Men of all ages and races volunteered to serve, taking on a variety of military roles. Women, too, did their part, volunteering as nurses or taking on responsibilities at home, including factory work. Even those who did not go to work for the war effort helped by growing gardens, canning and making goods stretch a bit further. People who couldn't serve gathered metals and rubber for recycling, knitted socks for the troops, or helped to care for war veterans who returned injured from the front.

African-Americans were, initially, only able to serve in limited support capacities. While these roles were essential, they failed to take advantage of the bravery or skills of African-American troops. As the war continued, this changed and many African-American soldiers and airmen showed their valor in combat, particularly the Redtails or Tuskegee Airmen. While serving in Europe, African-American servicemen were treated, by the local people, as equals. On the home front, the defense industry was desegregated by executive order; however, segregation continued throughout World War II in the Armed Forces.

While women's contribution is often remembered at home, women also served overseas in large numbers. Many, but not all, were nurses, working in field hospitals in Europe. Their role was essential in helping to preserve the health of the troops and providing comfort. Other women took on roles as office staff or even as translators. At home, women are often remembered with the image of "Rosie the Riveter," the woman who has set aside her skirts for a coverall and tied up her hair to go to work in the factory, building goods needed for war.

The United States also tapped into another population during Selective Service Registration. While the draft is commonly associated with young men, men up to age 64 registered with Selective Service, noting any skills, knowledge or industrial ability. Older men who had retired or moved on to new careers took on roles they had left behind or returned to the work force to provide assistance with the war effort.

Throughout America, everyone worked to support the war by buying war bonds or collecting for the Red Cross and other agencies. Even children helped to collect pennies to donate to the Red Cross to help the injured veterans or prisoners of war.

In a great many ways, World War II united America like it had never been. Faced with a common enemy, America, for a time, moved beyond at least some judgments on the base of race or gender.

SAMPLE LONG ESSAY

Franklin Roosevelt was elected on a series of big campaign promises, including banking reform, job creation and help for the people of America. He was successful with all of these campaign promises, creating the New Deal. The New Deal incorporated all of these programs, in an attempt to bring the country out of the Great Depression.

The New Deal relied upon a specific economic theory, called Keynesian Economics. This theory stated that during times of economic recession, the government should incur debt through job creation and other types of government spending to improve the economy. While some critics consider the New Deal to be a form of socialism, it is, by definition, not. Socialism requires government ownership of means of production, as well as intentional redistribution of wealth.

Many New Deal programs created jobs by investing in the infrastructure of the country, from utilities to roads to schools to national parks. This job creation put Americas back to work, provided a living wage and allowed them to support their families. The government did not, in this case, own any means of production, but simply opted to spend on community-oriented projects of various sort. This type of spending is traditionally associated with state and federal governments, as these are not private property. Other New Deal programs focused on the production of specific items for the government, including works of art and written materials. Again, these are jobs-for-hire, rather than any form of government ownership or redistribution of wealth.

The New Deal also created Social Security to provide cash payments for the elderly and disabled. This was intended to protect some of the most vulnerable in society. While social welfare programs may, in some cases, qualify as socialism, Social Security is funded through individual paycheck deductions. This, by definition, is not socialism. It is, in fact, closer to a public pension program managed by the federal government. Individuals receive payments, unless they are disabled children, based upon wages they have paid into social security during their careers.

The New Deal was designed to meet an urgent need, to provide jobs, reduce unemployment and protect the lives of Americans across the country. These jobs enabled them to buy consumer goods once again. While the New Deal provided immediate relief, it did not fully end the Depression; that occurred with the beginning of World War II.

Made in the USA
Middletown, DE
05 February 2021